The Citizen's Guide to the Law

How to Handle
Routine Legal Matters
Involving:
- Business Law and Contracts
- Estate Planning
- Probate
- Will Writing

John C. Howell

Library of Congress Cataloging in Publication Data

HOWELL, JOHN COTTON, 1926-
   The citizen's guide to the law.

   (A Spectrum Book)
   Previously published as: Legal guide for laymen.
1979.
     1. Law—United States—Popular works.   I. Title.
KF387.H63   349.73   81-752
ISBN 0-13-134619-9 (pbk.)   AACR2

The forms contained in this book have been carefully selected in order to cover the situations and problems of the subject matter as completely as possible. They will be useful to lawyers for adaptations to specific situations in connection with which they are to be used. Laymen will find them informative on the contingencies and problems which should be considered, but should consult their own legal counsel before entering into any contract or business arrangement based on these forms.

This publication is designed to provide accurate and authoritative information in regard to the subject matter covered. It is sold with the understanding that the publisher is not engaged in rendering legal, accounting or other professional service. If legal advice or other expert assistance is required, the services of a competent professional person should be sought.

—From a Declaration of Principles jointly
adopted by a Committee of the American Bar
Association and a Committee of Publishers.

For the purposes of editorial simplification, this publication generally uses the masculine pronoun in the generic sense, to indicate *person*. The author and the publisher are fully aware that the information in this volume pertains to women as well as men, and no discrimination is implied or intended.

Printed in the United States of America

PRENTICE-HALL INTERNATIONAL, INC., *London*
PRENTICE-HALL OF AUSTRALIA PTY. LIMITED, *Sydney*
PRENTICE-HALL OF CANADA, LTD., *Toronto*
PRENTICE-HALL OF INDIA PRIVATE LIMITED, *New Delhi*
PRENTICE-HALL OF JAPAN, INC., *Tokyo*
PRENTICE-HALL OF SOUTHEAST ASIA PTE. LTD., *Singapore*
WHITEHALL BOOKS LIMITED, *Wellington, New Zealand*

Contents

Preface

Most American citizens are generally intimidated when they get involved with the "law" and with "lawyers." Neither the law nor the lawyers should be thought of as so imposing, majestic or enigmatic. While it is true that many lawyers try to be abstruse and inscrutable and many laws, especially those from the federal bureaucrats in Washington, D.C., are quite incomprehensible to most people, the "law" is defined as nothing more than a set of rules by which we govern ourselves. This is, of course, a simplistic overstatement of the point that we, as American citizens, elect the lawmakers and are responsible for their acts, including the laws they enact. Whatever resistance you may have to this concept, it is true that we, as voters, are supposed to be in touch with our lawmakers, and that they are supposed to enact only those laws that we want!

Although we may not wish to take too much direct responsibility for the activities of our elected officials, we do have another choice: we can learn more about our laws, learn more about the people who enforce them, and learn more about lawyers. Moreover, we can change the laws.

This guide will give you a complete introduction to the law; it is a virtual law school course on understanding the law. The fascinating story about the development of law will captivate you, excite the history "buff" in you, and may well motivate you to look further into the activities of Hammurabi, Justinian, Marcus Aurelius, Alexander the Great, and others who shaped and fashioned the course of law and of history.

Learning about the development of law is not only interesting, but it is fun and can be most rewarding for those who want to know why the human being, as an individual, and society as a whole, do the things they do; and why we have so many laws that are designed to control so many activities and subjects.

The early part of this guide gives you a review of the three major areas of law: tort, contract and criminal. These discussions are brief because of space limitations; however, the coverage of business law, estate planning, avoiding probate, and will writing are all very pragmatic and realistic subjects in terms of your being able to handle many of the routine legal matters that you thought always required a lawyer.

You not only learn how to handle many legal matters yourself, but you can learn enough about a specific legal problem to put yourself in a controlling position when you hire a lawyer to represent you in a particular case. You should not be intimidated by lawyers. On the contrary, a lawyer is employed to render you services, and you are entitled to the services you pay for. You will be able to accomplish this only if you know enough about the law to control your lawyer.

The Citizens Law Library is designed to assist people in helping themselves in those legal matters that they can handle themselves, and to help them communicate with their lawyer effectively in those cases where a lawyer is required. We invite you to communicate with us if there are other legal subjects you wish to have included in the Citizens Law Library series.

The Complete Guide to Business Contracts
Corporate Executive's Legal Handbook
Estate Planning for the Small Business Owner
The Layman's Complete Guide to Forming a Corporation In Any State
Prepare Your Own Partnership Agreements
The Citizen's Guide to the Law
The Landlord-Tenant Relationship: The Citizen's Legal Guide
No-Fault Divorce: The Citizen's Legal Guide
Probate: The Citizen's Legal Guide
Writing a Will: The Citizen's Legal Guide
You Can Be Your Own Lawyer in Court: The Citizen's Legal Guide

1

The Development of Law

What Is Law?

The term "law," in its generic sense, means a rule of action or conduct duly prescribed by controlling authority, by the law-making power of the state, by the sovereign power, or by the supreme power of the state.

The law is that which is laid down, ordained, or established; a rule or method according to which phenomena or actions co-exist or follow each other; that which must be obeyed and followed by citizens, subject to sanctions or legal consequences.

An act of the legislature deposited in the office of the secretary of state, properly authenticated by presiding officers of the two houses, and approved by the governor, is law. It is a body of principles, standards and rules promulgated by government.

Law is nothing else than reason; law is the body of rules by which we govern ourselves. The law of a state is found in its statutory and constitutional enactments as interpreted by its courts, and, in the absence of statutory law, in the rulings of its courts. The law of the United

States is found in its Constitution, the Acts of Congress, and in its treaties all as interpreted by its courts, and in those matters specially committed to the judicial power of the rulings of its courts.

Justice Oliver Wendell Holmes said:

> The rational study of law is . . . to a large extent the study of history.
>
> *   *   *
>
> The life of the law has not been logic; it has been experience. The felt necessities of the time, the prevalent moral and political theories, intuitions of public policy, avowed or unconscious, even the prejudices which judges share with their fellow man have had a good deal more to do than the syllogism in determining the rules by which men should be governed.

Blackstone gave a more formalistic definition of the term "law." He called it:

> A rule of civil conduct prescribed by the supreme power of a state, commanding what is right and prohibiting what is wrong. And, first, it is a rule: not a transient sudden order from a superior to or concerning a particular person; but something permanent, uniform and universal. [Blackstone's Commentaries]

Blackstone's definition does not fit our present day standards, at least to the extent that it makes law depend upon the supreme power of the state. Blackstone's definition is not compatible with the genius of our form of government; neither is it literally true as applicable to our system. In our system of jurisprudence we acknowledge no supreme power, except that of the people.

Another interesting (and puzzling) definition of the term law is as follows:

A law may be defined as an assemblage of signs declarative of a volition concerned or adopted by the sovereign in a state, concerning the conduct to be observed in a certain case by a certain person or class of persons, who in the case in question are or are supposed to be subject to his power: such volition trusting for its accomplishment to the expectation of certain events which it is intended such declarative should upon occasion by a means of bringing to pass, and the prospect of which it is intended should act as a motive upon those whose conduct is in question.

The term "natural law" was an expression largely used in the philosophical speculations of the Roman jurists of the Antoine Age, and was intended to denote a system of rules and principles for the guidance of human conduct which, independent of enacted law or of the system peculiar to any one people, might be discovered by the rational intelligence of man, and would be found to grow out of and conform to his nature.

It has been said that natural law is a rule which so necessarily agrees with the nature and state of man that, without observing its maxims, the peace and happiness of society can never be preserved.

Law, then, is a set of rules by which a society governs itself.

Historical Background and Development of Law

Even before men could write, the laws and customs of each community were passed down from one generation

3

to the next by the older members of the group. That's a long time ago, but when you think it through you can find that the beginning of the history of law is precisely the same date as the dawn of the history of mankind. With some reflection, you will recognize that you can't name one instance in which any "society" or group of men and women lived any significant period of time without laws or rules. And whether the source of the laws happened to be some "chief," a "witch doctor," a bloody dictator, the gods of the sky, the Bible, or from some place known as heaven, there is one truth that emerges with the ineluctability of a syllogism: laws are made to encourage us to do what is "good," and avoid that which is "bad." If you want to know how to distinguish between that which is good and that which is bad, just close your eyes, relax, and ask your conscience. You can't miss.

> The law is the witness and external deposit of our moral life. Its history is the history of the moral development of the race. [Justice Oliver Wendell Holmes]

Code of Hammurabi

The earliest law which has been preserved is the one developed about 2000 B.C. by Hammurabi, a ruler of the ancient Sumerians. The Sumerians lived in the valleys of the Tigris and Euphrates rivers. Hammurabi's Code set forth a complete system of law; it set down the kinds of punishment to be used for a variety of offenses; and it established the amounts of payment to be made for various services rendered. If you are a student of history you will be amazed at how "smart" the people were who inhabited the earth 4000 years ago. You can look it up!

The Law of Moses

About 1200 B.C., Moses, a Hebrew, hammered out the Ten Commandments, which stated principles of behavior that had long been recognized as good. These Commandments, in one form or another, have had a profound influence on every body of law during all ages of history.

The Law of the Ancient Greeks

The Greeks were among the first to introduce the idea that laws are made by men and can therefore be changed by men whenever the need arises. This idea marked a great step forward in human thought. Before that time, people believed that laws always came from a god or group of gods. They thought that these divine laws were revealed through the rulers or priests and could not be changed by men, even though they may have been unjust.

The Greeks respected law more than any other people had done before. They believed that a country should be ruled by law rather than by men; this basic concept is becoming more elusive for us in our modern society.

Law in Ancient Rome

The Romans made great strides in the development of the law. Roman law was more complete, and it was in Rome that the first legal profession developed. The first important step in Roman law came in 450 B.C., when the Law of the Twelve Tables, based on the Roman religion, was prepared by a council of ten men. The laws were inscribed on brass tablets, and for hundreds of years many Romans memorized the Twelve Tablets, and the laws were passed from generation to generation.

Modern European Law

The influence of Roman law declined after the fall of the Roman Empire; however, the ideas developed by the Roman and canon law during the Middle Ages still had a profound influence on the laws of most European countries. The Code Napolean has also had a great influence in modern-day laws. The Code Napoleon was originally made up of thirty-six laws brought together under the direction of Napoleon Bonaparte, who in 1803 directed outstanding law writers to collect and simplify into one statement the laws by which France was governed. The Code was completed in 1804, and forms the foundation upon which the whole body of French law is now based. It has had a great influence on the laws of many countries in Western Europe.

American Law

When the English colonists settled in North America, they brought with them the English common law, which formed the basis for American and Canadian law.

Common law comprises the body of those principles and rules of action, relating to the government and security of persons and property, which derive their authority solely from usages and customs of immemorial antiquity, or from the judgments and decrees of the courts recognizing, affirming, and enforcing such usages and customs. It is the legal embodiment of practice and common sense whose guiding star is to do what is right.

The nature of the common law requires that each time a rule of law is applied, it be carefully scrutinized to make sure that the conditions and needs of the times have not so changed as to make further application of it the instrument of injustice. Whenever an old rule is found unsuited to present conditions or is unsound, it should be set aside and a rule declared which is in harmony with those conditions and meets the demands of justice. Justice Cardozo said:

> A rule which in its origin was the creation of the courts themselves, and was supposed in the making to express the mores of the day, may be abrogated by courts when the mores have so changed that perpetuation of the rule would do violence to the social conscience . . . This is not usurpation. It is not even innovation. It is the reservation for ourselves of the same power of creation that built up the common law through its exercise by the judges of the past.

7

The Legal System in America

The English common law has been adopted as the basis of jurisprudence in all the states in the United States except Louisiana, where the civil law (Code of Napoleon) prevails in civil matters. The U.S. Constitution and the constitutions of the 50 states form the foundations upon which our laws are based.

The U.S. Constitution establishes the three branches of the federal government, executive, legislative, and judicial, and it establishes the balance of power among those three branches. It sets forth the powers granted to the federal government and the powers reserved to the states. Thus, the U.S. Constitution states what cases the federal courts have jurisdiction to handle and leaves all other judicial power to the states.

Whatever may be said, in an historical sense, about the "balance of power" among the three federal branches of government and the powers reserved to the states, it is plain to most knowledgeable citizens that the federal government has taken unto itself, during the past 45 years, a preponderating and dominant share of all governmental activities into every aspect of our lives. There is scarcely any aspect of our daily lives that does not get exposed to the searching light of federal governmental intervention.

All powers not granted by the U.S. Constitution to our federal government are reserved to the states.

Constitutional Law

The basic and fundamental laws of our land are found in the federal and state constitutions. It is far more difficult to change the constitution than it is to enact or change other laws. The U.S. Constitution may be amended in two ways: (1) two-thirds of the members of both houses of Congress may propose amendments, or (2) on the application of the legislatures of two-thirds of the states, Congress may call a convention for proposing amendments.

Any changes must be ratified by three-fourths of the states or by special conventions in three-fourths of the states.

Each of the state constitutions sets out the basic governmental structure of executive, legislative and judicial branches. Each of these governmental branches perform certain functions within the guidelines set out in the constitutions.

Statutory Law

The legislatures of each state are the law-making branches of the state, and the U.S. Congress is the legislative body of the federal government. Each state has a state legislature and local county and city governments.

Most of the legislative bodies of the states are divided into two parts or houses, often called the Senate and House of Representatives, as in the U.S. Congress, whose members are elected for different terms. Each house must enact a bill before it is sent to the executive to be signed into law, or vetoed. The federal and state constitutions provide for the enactment of a bill notwithstanding the veto of the executive branch if a sufficiently large majority of the legislature vote in favor of the bill. This process is known as overriding a veto. Laws passed by state legislatures are called statutes; those enacted by the local governments are usually called ordinances.

Any law passed by the legislative branch may be reviewed by the judicial branch of the government if someone affected by the law asserts that it is contrary to the state or federal constitution. If a court with proper jurisdiction finds that a law is unconstitutional, it becomes inoperative. The power of the courts to examine the constitutionality of laws passed by the legislature is called the right of judicial review. It is one of the strongest weapons that citizens have in protecting their constitutional rights. The U.S. Supreme Court has been very liberal during the past 20 to 40 years in construing the constitution to protect the private rights of the people.

Executive

We usually think of the executive branch of government as that magnificent group of workers presided over by our president, the governor, or the mayor. These are the chief executives of that branch of government. The chief executive is usually an elected official who holds office for a term of years specified in the constitution or charter. It is the responsibility of the executive branch to propose new laws to the legislature, to approve or disapprove laws that have been passed, and to enforce the statutes that are in effect. It is the job of the executive to see that the government operates to protect the interests of the people. While the executive branch has no power to pass laws, it does set up regulatory and administrative agencies; these are the bodies that proliferate like crab grass and look over you all the time.

Administrative Law

Administrative law is an area of law that holds a special fascination for me; I have been personally involved in the operation of many of the federal and state agencies. Many of the agencies proceeded on the basis that "more regulation" is good government!

The term "administrative law," while well recognized by judicial and other authorities, having given rise to an enormous literature and decision-making rulings, has no authoritative definition in English. In one sense the term embraces everything that the law controls, or is intended to control; it is the vast network encompassing the administrative operations of government, including the laws which provide for the structure of government and prescribe its procedure. It embraces the law which

11

governs the methods of legislatures, provides for the existence and operation of the courts, the agencies themselves, and governs their procedure, and determines personnel policies in all branches of the government. Administrative law is concerned with the protection of private rights, and the problems of administrative regulations rather than those of administrative management.

Administrative law is involved in the legal problems arising out of the existence of agencies which combine in a single entity the legislative, executive, and judicial powers of government. Even though the civics teachers and the law professors may still claim that the three branches of our federal government are "separate" and "balanced," the administrative agencies do all three with the sweeping power of an emperor.

The primary function of administrative agencies and administrative law is to carry into effect the will of the federal or state government as expressed by its legislature, but one of the most striking facts upon a realistic view of administrative agencies generally is the variety of their specific functions; they get involved in every aspect of human activity.

Some of these functions vested in particular administrative agencies embrace those of the legislature, the grand jury, the prosecutor, the policeman, and the courts, and some statutory schemes provide for or permit administrative enforcement. This is what some people refer to as being "prosecutor, judge and jury." For example, the Federal Trade Commission has recently been under severe criticism for its alleged arbitrary and unbridled usurpation and misuse of power.

Case Law

Decisions rendered by the various courts are sometimes referred to as legal precedents; that is, they become a rule of law to apply to the case before the court and to future cases. Judges are, of course, bound by the constitutions, statutes and laws of the land, but there are so many new laws, new cases, and controversies that the judges are grossly overworked in trying to resolve disputes that arise among the citizens. Many modern judges do not pay too much attention to precedents. Some courts make more new laws than the legislative branches. The so-called "Warren Court" set the stage during the 1950s and 1960s for other courts to ignore legal precedents, and to set out on a course of "liberal" interpretations of the constitutions and statutes to conform to the current popular political ideas of the day. This intrusion of the federal government into the private lives of the citizens, along with the expansion of legislative and executive interference into the private rights of people, has brought into question the competency of our government to properly govern.

The Court System

Federal Courts

The federal system consists of the following courts:

1. United States Supreme Court.
2. Eleven U.S. Courts of Appeals.
3. U.S. District Courts (at least one in each state).
4. Other courts including U.S. Court of Customs and Patent Appeals, U.S. Court of Claims, Tax Court of the United States, U.S. Customs Court, and U.S. Court of Military Appeals.

These courts have jurisdiction in the following:

1. Cases in law and equity arising under the U.S. Constitution, the laws of the United States and treaties—called "federal question jurisdiction." [28 U.S.C. 1331]
2. Cases affecting ambassadors, counsels, etc.
3. Cases of admiralty and maritime jurisdiction.
4. Cases to which the U.S. is a party.
5. Controversies between two or more states, or between a state and a citizen of another state.
6. Controversies between citizens of different states—diversity jurisdiction—or between citizens of foreign nations. [28 U.S.C. 1332]

State Courts

The state court systems vary greatly in the patterns, names, and organizations of courts; however, they fall into the following broad groups:

1. State Court of Last Resort, generally called Supreme Court, Court of Appeals, Supreme Judicial Court, Su-

14

preme Court of Errors, and other similar names.

2. Intermediate Appellate Courts called by various names.
3. Trial Courts of General Jurisdiction.
4. Trial Courts of Limited or Special Jurisdiction.
5. Local Trial Courts sometimes called Traffic Court, Police Court, Small Claims Court, Justice of the Peace Court, Alderman's Court, Magistrate Court, Town Court, Parish Court, Mayor's Court, etc.

The "subject matter" (what kind of cases the court can decide) of state trial courts varies from state to state, but the general pattern is to have:

1. A trial court of general jurisdiction usually called Superior Court, District Court, Circuit Court, and other names. This is the *main* trial court in the state.
2. Courts of "limited" or special jurisdiction—usually a civil court that handles cases involving amounts up to specified amounts—typically $5,000 to $10,000. Special probate courts, juvenile courts, domestic relations courts, small claims courts, Justice Courts, Magistrate Court, and Mayor's Court are examples of other names given to these courts.

Laws come from many sources including (1) the U.S. Constitution, (2) federal statutes and treaties, (3) federal administrative agencies and bodies, (4) the federal courts, (5) the state constitutions, statutes, court decisions, and administrative agencies, (6) your local governments, and (7) international law.

2

The Law of Torts

What Is a Tort?

Tort is a legal concept possessing the basic element of a wrong with resultant injury and consequential damage which is cognizable in a court of law. Actually, this is another word that the courts call "impossible" to define with precision. It is that great body of law described generally as a civil wrong. Examples of torts are personal injury auto accidents, libel and slander, malicious prosecution, and other personal and property types of hurt. A tort is a legal wrong committed upon the person or property independent of contract. It may be either a direct invasion of some legal right of the individual, an infraction of some public duty by which special damage accrues to the individual, or the violation of some private obligation by which damages accrue.

Certain acts may be torts and crimes, simultaneously. There is, however, a significant legal difference between a tort and a crime. A tort is a civil wrong against an individual; a crime is an offense against the public at large, or, as the judges call it, an offense against the peace and

17

dignity of the sovereign state. A crime is a wrongful act against society.

When an act is committed that constitutes a crime, the state prosecutor (usually called district attorney or county attorney) has the responsibility to investigate, assemble evidence, bring criminal charges, and conduct the trial of the person charged. The same act may also constitute a tort against an individual, who can bring a civil action against the tort feasor to collect damages in a court of law.

Elements of a Tort

The three elements of every tort action are: (1) the existence of a legal duty from the defendant to the plaintiff; (2) breach of that duty; and (3) damage as a proximate result.

A tort is usually thought of as an act or action which causes physical injury to you personally, results in damage to your property, or deprives you of your personal liberty and freedom, where such act or action is committed without just cause.

Kinds of Torts

There are two broad classifications of torts, (1) intentional and (2) unintentional, or accidental. These will be discussed separately.

Intentional Torts

An intentional tort is a willful act; it is an act that implies an intent or purpose to injure or hurt. It is an act which proceeds from a conscious motion of the will, a voluntary act.

False Imprisonment. This is the unlawful restraint by one person of the physical liberty of another. The word false in this phrase is synonymous with, and means, unlawful. A state statutory definition of false imprisonment is that it is "the unlawful violation of the personal liberty of another," and, under these statutes, whether the offense is treated either as a tort or a crime, or as both, the definition is the same.

Some courts have said that false imprisonment consists of a direct restraint without adequate legal justification. The gist of the act is lack of lawful authority. The offense is regarded as a trespass to the person.

Malicious Prosecution. An action or proceeding begun in malice, without probable cause to believe it can succeed, and that finally ends in failure. As applied to the cause of action, it is a suit for damages brought by one against whom a criminal prosecution, civil suit, or other legal proceeding has been instituted maliciously and without probable cause, after the termination of the first proceedings in favor of the defendant therein. The gist of the action is the putting of legal process in force regularly for the mere purpose of vexation or injury.

19

In general, to authorize the maintenance of an action for malicious prosecution, the following elements must be shown: (1) the institution or continuation of original judicial proceedings, either civil or criminal, or of administrative or disciplinary proceedings; (2) by, or at the instance of, the defendant; (3) the termination of such proceedings in the plaintiff's favor; (4) malice in instituting the proceedings; (5) want of probable cause for the proceeding; and (6) the suffering of injury or damage as a result of the prosecution or proceedings.

Abuse of Process. This tort consists of the malicious misuse or misapplication of that process to accomplish some purpose not warranted or commanded by the writ. In brief, it is the malicious perversion of a regularly issued civil or criminal process, for a purpose and to obtain a result not lawfully warranted or properly attainable thereby, and for which perversion an action will lie to recover the pecuniary loss sustained.

The essential elements of abuse of process are (1) that the defendant made an illegal, improper, perverted use of the process, a use neither warranted nor authorized by the process, (2) that the defendant had an ulterior motive or purpose in exercising such illegal, perverted, or improper use of process, and (3) that damage resulted to the plaintiff from the irregularity.

Assault and Battery. Personal injury is the term frequently used to describe torts to the body. Usually these are accidental, but not always; some are planned that way. Assault and battery is one of them. These are, as you may guess, two of the oldest torts known to mankind. Like the history of law, these started with the dawn of civilization. An assault is an open threat of bodily contact with someone, without his permission. The actual contact is a battery.

A tort action for damages resulting from an assault and battery is to recover damages, such as medical expenses, hospital costs, and the like. One may also collect damages for mental distress in addition to the physical hurt. This is called by some courts an injury caused by the touching of the mind, not of the body. Damages would include compensation for mental upset, fright, humiliation and for any physical illness that may result. Most folks also think of criminal prosecution in connection with these torts.

Invasion of Privacy. The right of privacy is the right to be free from the unwarranted appropriation or exploitation of one's personality, the publicizing of one's private affairs with which the public has no legitimate concern, or the wrongful intrusion into one's private activities in such manner as to outrage or cause mental suffering, shame or humiliation to a person of ordinary sensibilities. It is the right to be let alone, to be free from unwarranted publicity, and to live without unwarranted interference by the public in matters with which the public is not necessarily concerned.

The law recognizes four forms of invasion of privacy: (1) intrusion upon the person's seclusion and solitude, or into his private affairs; (2) public disclosure of embarrassing private facts about the person; (3) publicity which places the person in a false light in the public eye; and (4) appropriation for another's advantage, of the person's name or likeness.

Defamation. Defamation is the taking from one's reputation, the offense of injuring a person's character, fame, or reputation by false and malicious statements. The term includes both libel and slander.

The distinction between "criticism" and "defamation" is that criticism deals only with such things as invite public attention or call for public comment, and does not follow a man into his private life, or pry into his domestic concerns, and it never attacks the individual, but only his work or ideas.

The fundamental differences between a right to "privacy" and a right to freedom from "defamation" is that the former directly concerns one's own peace of mind, whereas the latter concerns primarily one's reputation.

Libel. Libel is a method of defamation expressed by print, writing, pictures, or signs, and publication that is injurious to the reputation of another. Defamatory words read aloud by a speaker from written articles and broadcast by radio constitutes libel.

Libel is an accusation in writing or printing against the character of a person which affects his reputation, in that it tends to hold him up to hatred, abuse, ridicule, contempt, shame, disgrace, or obloquy, to degrade him in the estimation of the community, to induce an evil opinion of him in the minds of other persons, to make him an object of reproach, to diminish his respectability or abridge his comforts, to change his position in society for the worse, to dishonor or discredit him in the estimation of the public or his friends and acquaintances, or to deprive him of friendly intercourse in society, or cause him to be shunned or avoided, or where it is charged that one has violated his public duty as a public officer.

Slander. Slander is the speaking of base and defamatory words intended to prejudice another in his reputation, office, trade, business, or means of livelihood. Both libel and slander are methods of defamation, the former being expressed by print, writings, pictures or signs, the latter orally. An essential element of slander is that slanderous words be spoken in the presence of another person than the person slandered, and publication is always a material and issuable fact in an action for slander. In other words, if you print libelous words on a piece of paper and no other person sees or reads it, there is no defamation; if you say slanderous words but no person hears it, this is not slander. There must be a publication.

Torts Against Real Property

Trespass. The term trespass in its broadest sense is the doing of an unlawful act or of lawful acts in an unlawful manner to the injury of another's person or property. It is an unlawful act committed with violence, actual or implied, causing injury to the person, property, or relative rights of another; an injury or misfeasance to the person, property or rights of another, done with force and violence, either actual or implied in law. It comprehends not only forceable wrongs, but also acts whose consequences make them tortious.

It has been said that trespass, in its most comprehensive sense, signifies any transgression or offense against the law of nature, of society, or of the country in which we live; and this, whether it relates to a man's person or to his property. In its more limited and ordinary sense, it signifies an injury committed with violence, and this violence may be either actual or implied; and the law will imply violence even though none is actually used when the injury is of a direct and immediate kind, and committed on the person or tangible and corporeal property of the plaintiff. Assault and battery is an instance of actual violence. Implied violence is a peaceable but wrongful entry upon a person's land.

Fraud and Deceit

It has been said that the fertility of man's invention in devising new schemes of fraud is so great that the courts

24

have declined to define the term fraud and deceit, lest the craft of men should find ways to committing fraud which might evade such a definition. However, the law professors and writers have given it a shot. It means deceitful practices in depriving or endeavoring to deprive another of his known right by means of some artful device or plan contrary to the plain rules of common honesty; unfair dealing; a positive act resulting from a willful intent to deceive; anything which is calculated to deceive, whether it is a single act or a combination of circumstances, or acts or words which amount to a suppression of the truth, or mere silence. With these guidelines, you might say it means whatever a judge or jury says it means in any given case. In all events it is a tort, and where you are caused damages as a result thereof, you can bring a lawsuit to seek damages.

Unintentional (Accidental) Torts

Negligence is the omission of some act which a reasonable man, guided by those ordinary considerations which ordinarily regulate human affairs, would do, or the doing of something which a reasonable and prudent man would not do. It is characterized by inadvertence, thoughtlessness, inattention, and the like, while "wantonness or recklessness" is characterized by willfulness. The law of negligence is founded on reasonable conduct or reasonable care under all circumstances of the particular case. The doctrine of negligence rests on the duty of every person to exercise due care in his conduct toward others when there is a possibility that injury may result. Negligence is not necessarily intentional conduct; inaction as well as action may be negligence.

Negligence is the failure to exercise ordinary care; the breach of legal duty. It usually consists in the involuntary and casual, that is, accidental, doing or omission of something which results in an injury; it is synonymous with heedlessness, carelessness, thoughtlessness, disregard, inattention, inadvertence, remissness and oversight.

Some courts have suggested that there are various degrees or kinds of negligence: culpable, gross, ordinary, criminal, hazardous, passive, slight, wanton, willful, and others. In the end, it's all a jury question.

Proximate Cause

This term is most difficult to define; it is that which, in a natural and continuous sequence, unbroken by any efficient intervening cause, produces the injury, and without which the result would not have occurred. It is that which is nearest in the order of responsible causation, that which stands next in causation to the effect, not necessarily in time or space but in causal relation. Proximate cause is the last negligent act contributory to an injury, without which such injury would not have resulted. It is the dominant cause, the moving or producing cause, or the efficient cause; the one that necessarily sets the other causes in operation.

Proximate cause is different from "immediate cause." The immediate cause is generally referred to in the law as the nearest cause in point of time and space, while an act or omission may be the proximate cause of an injury without being the immediate cause. Thus, where several causes combine to produce an injury, the last intervening cause is commonly referred to as the immediate cause, although some other agency more remote in time or space may, in causal relation, be the nearer to the result, and thus be the proximate responsible cause.

Contributory Negligence

This is an act or omission amounting to want of ordinary care on the part of the complaining party, which, concurring with the defendant's negligence, is the proximate cause of an injury. It is the want of ordinary care on the part of the person injured, which combined and concurred with the defendant's negligence, and contributed to the injury as a proximate cause thereof, and as an element without which the injury would not have occurred.

It is the negligent act of the plaintiff which, concurring and cooperating with the negligent act of the defendant, becomes real, efficient, and proximate cause of the injury, or the cause without which the injury would not have occurred.

At one time the contributory negligence of a plaintiff would bar any recovery from the defendant; however, in most states, by statute and court decision, this is no longer the law. The doctrine of comparative negligence has been adopted in many states; negligence on the part of the plaintiff only diminishes the amount of damages he can collect.

Comparative Negligence

The rule of comparative negligence is that contributory negligence of the person injured will not be a complete bar to recovery, but that there shall be an apportionment of responsibility, or of damages in accordance with the relative fault of the parties.

The question of whether there is fault on the part of either or both parties and the apportionment of each, the percentage of fault for each, is a jury question. This rule was adopted to ease the hardships and rigors of the common law rule of contributory negligence, where even the slightest degree of negligence (even 1 percent) would bar an injured person from recovery.

Some comparative negligence statutes provide that if the injured party's negligence is equal or greater than the defendant's negligence, he is barred from recovery. The modern trend, by statutes, court rules and decisions, jury verdicts, and otherwise, is to be more liberal in permitting injured parties to recover from someone. For example, there has been a proposal by some advocates for the enactment of statutes that compensate innocent victims of crimes.

No Fault Liabilities

There are a long series of legal doctrines in our current law that impose liability upon persons irrespective of whether they may be at fault. Three examples follow.

1. *Workmen's Compensation.* This is liability imposed by statute, where the workers are covered by workmen's compensation which provides for compensation for injuries incurred on the job without regard to the negligence of anyone. This is currently the law in all states.

2. *Products Liability* (imposed by statute). Some states and the federal government have enacted legislation that creates liability irrespective of the element of negligence. This is "social" legislation that seems to be compatible with the ideas of "modern" government.

3. *Warranty of Habitability* (in landlord-tenant relationships). This is a rule of law that has emerged during the past five or ten years. Essentially, it is that as a matter of law a landlord warrants that the rented premises are habitable. Here is the way one court stated the rule:

> In our opinion the above considerations demonstrate convincingly that in a rental of an apartment as a dwelling unit, be it a written or oral lease, for a specified time or at will, there is an implied warranty of habitability by the landlord that the apartment is habitable and fit for living. This means that at the inception of the rental there are no latent defects in facilities vital to the use of the premises for residential purposes and that these essential facilities will remain during the entire term in a condition which makes the property livable. . . . The warranty of

habitability which we hold exists in such a case is imposed of law on the basis of public policy. It arises by operation of law because of the relationship of the parties, the nature of the transaction, and the surrounding circumstances [Kline v. Burns, 276 A.2d 248, 251, 252 (New Hampshire)]

This is currently the law in most states, either by statute or by case law. It is believed that it will be the law in virtually all states within the next few years.

No Fault Insurance

The concept of the traditional tort liability in automobile accident cases has proven quite inadequate for a number of reasons, some of which are that (1) contributory negligence barred all recovery in the beginning; (2) the comparative negligence theory—adopted to soften the rigors of no recovery at all—proved almost impossible to administer; (3) the lawyers, doctors and insurance companies—their agents and employees—ended up getting most of the money; (4) the delays in court cases were interminable, most cases taking several years to get any money from judgments or settlements; (5) the system was an open invitation to fraud by lawyers, adjustors, investigators, claimants, judges, doctors, medical assistants, ambulance drivers, and others; and (6) the system was fundamentally unsound and inefficient and failed to accomplish its objectives.

Some states have adopted the so-called "No Fault" statutes, which permit reparations for automobile accident losses to be made independently of a fault determination. These plans are really only partial self-insurance plans. The federal government brought great pressure on the states to adopt these plans as recommended in official studies made by the Department of Transportation (one of your administrative agencies).

The National Conference of Commissioners on Uniform State Laws drafted a proposed statute for the states providing for a no fault automobile reparations system. It is called "Uniform Motor Vehicle Accident Reparations Act."

There have been a number of other plans by insurance companies, lawyers, "citizens" groups sponsored by insurance companies (or lawyers), and others. Essentially there are two main features of the proposals that are significantly different from the tort system based on fault. The first is that regardless of legal fault, an insured motorist who suffers injury from an automobile accident shall receive compensation (reparations, they call it), from his or her own insurance company. The second difference is that tort liability is abolished, at least to the extent of the benefits received.

The purpose of most no fault plans is to afford reparations, or at least partial reparations, for the objectively provable economic losses resulting from automobile accidents. Typically, the statutes eliminate or curtail the payment of benefits for items of general damage such as pain and suffering. However, most no fault statutes retain conventional tort liability as the basis for reparations in cases of serious injury, dismemberment, or the like. This was, of course, a compromise essential to get the statutes adopted.

It has been said by some writers that the practical effect of the adoption of personal injury protection insurance is to afford the citizen the security of prompt and certain recovery to a fixed amount of the most salient elements of his out-of-pocket expenses and an increased flexibility in avoiding duplicate coverage, at double premiums, for the same expenses. In return for this, he surrenders the possibly minimal damages for pain and suffering recoverable in cases not marked by serious economic loss or objective indicia of grave injury, and also surrenders the outside chance that through a generous settlement or a liberal award by a judge or jury he may be able to reap a monetary windfall out of his misfortune.

It is my sad duty to tell you that the fraudulent and corrupt practitioners under the old system of laws have simply found new tricks and methods to continue their activities. The "human element," they call it!

3

Contract Law

What Is a Contract?

Lawyers, judges, professors, law students and writers spend a great deal of time talking, debating, arguing, and discussing the definition of contracts. It is easy to give a legal textbook definition, but the problem most of us have is determining whether a particular transaction comes within the definition. The professors define a contract as a promise, or set of promises, for breach of which the law gives a remedy, or for the performance of which the law in some way recognizes a duty. This is a little like saying a contract is a "contract" or a contract is a "valid agreement." The professors usually proceed to explain the essential elements of a contract. These are: (1) a valid offer; (2) an acceptance of the offer; (3) valid consideration; (4) legal capacity of the respective parties; (5) legal subject matter; and (6) a writing, if required by law (Statute of Frauds).

This description of a contract may not be as elusive as the "I know one when I see it" definition, but you should understand that the big problem results from the diffi-

33

culty that most people have in agreeing as to the "adequacy" or "sufficiency" of these essential elements of a contract.

Typically, a controversy can develop where two contracting parties agree that there must be "consideration" to have a legal contract, but they disagree as to what constitutes consideration in a given case. It is important for you, in negotiating and preparing your contracts, to be familiar with the general principles of contract law governing these elements of a contract.

Offer and Acceptance

An offer is the communication of one person (offeror) to another person (offeree) of an intent to enter into a mutual agreement based upon definite and certain terms. An offer may be revoked or withdrawn before acceptance by the offeree. An acceptance is simply a communication by the offeree to the offeror that the offer is accepted. The acceptance must be absolute and must be strictly in accord with the terms of the offer. If other conditions or terms are included in an attempted acceptance, it constitutes a counter offer for another contract. This is one of the "hot" items for litigation, because many people, after a long series of discussions and negotiations, tend to remember only those discussions involving their own ideas and thoughts. Put in more pragmatic terms, two people don't remember the same things from the same discussion!

In addition to the usual offer and acceptance to form a bilateral contract, there is what is called a unilateral contract, which consists of an offer in which the offeror does not receive a return promise as consideration for the contract, but receives something other than a promise of assent such as an act or performance.

Consideration

A dictionary definition of consideration as an essential element of a valid contract is "the inducement to a contract, or other legal transaction; an act or forebearance or the promise thereof done or given by one party in return for the act or promise of another." Many people think of consideration as a payment of money or other thing of value. A more legalistic definition is that consideration is a legal benefit to the promisor or a legal detriment to the promisee; it may be a forebearance or a creation, modification, or destruction of a legal relationship, or it may be a return promise.

Legal Capacity of Parties

Generally, any adult person has the legal capacity to enter into a valid contract. Incompetency, minority (usually under the age of 18), fraud and duress, or other such matters usually bring into question the capacity of parties to enter into contracts. The general description of a person in the community as a "crazy" does not necessarily make that person incompetent to enter into contracts. If a person understands the full nature of the transaction into which he is entering, the courts generally find legal capacity to contract.

Legal Subject Matter

A contract, to be enforceable by the courts, must involve legal subject matter or transactions. If an agreement relates to the doing of an illegal or unlawful act such as gambling (in most states) or violation of statutes, public policy or other laws, it is not legal, valid or enforceable. This is an often overlooked factor in preparing contracts; you should be alert to any transaction which may be contrary to zoning laws, permit requirements, consumer protection acts, the uniform commercial code, usury statutes, or other applicable laws and regulations.

**Statute of Frauds: Legal Requirement
that Certain Contracts Must Be in Writing**

As a general rule, oral or verbal agreements are valid, legal and enforceable. Even so, you probably know the importance of reducing all contracts to writing, and having them signed by the parties, and you should develop this habit in your business transactions. This simplifies the resolution of many disputes and differences that may occur. Where a dispute arises about contracts you will always be in a better position to support your case by the "best evidence" if you have it in writing.

The Statutes of Frauds, enacted in all states in this country, are based upon the old English statutes enacted in 1677 under the name of "An Act for the Prevention of Frauds and Perjuries." Although most of the provisions of the statutes have been repealed in England, except for land and guaranty contracts, the states have a wide variety of these statutes covering many topics. The usual subjects covered by the statutes include provisions that contracts to be valid must be in writing if they relate to (1) contracts for interests in land, (2) contracts that by the terms are not to be performed within one year after the making of the contract, and (3) contracts constituting a promise to answer for the debt, default, or miscarriage of another.

The Uniform Commercial Code requires certain personal property transactions to be in writing. Other types or classes of contracts may be included in these statutes, varying with individual states. There are many complicated exceptions to these statutes and rules, resulting from the very perplexing problem the lawmakers have in governing the question as to whether contracts should be in writing, and if so, which ones. Once you explore the complications involved in trying to apply these rules and exceptions, you will most certainly make most of your contracts in writing.

The subject of the Statutes of Frauds and discussions of the legal rules about having contracts in writing is beyond the scope of this book, but it is clear that you should strive to have a written contract in all important agreements you enter into.

Formation of Contracts:
Subject Matter and Governmental Control

Contracts are as easy to make as they are easy to break. Almost any manifestation of intent by the parties, verbal or written, will result in a valid contract so long as they have the elements that make up a contract.

A contract may be invalid or unenforceable because it violates public policy or some provision of a federal or state statute or ordinance, such as a prohibition against gambling, excessive interest, consumer acts, or regulatory rulings. The basic principle of law on this point is extremely important, and you should appreciate the significance and impact of the rule on all contracts. The rule was stated by the United States Supreme Court as follows:

> It is . . . settled that the laws which subsist at the time and place of the making of a contract, and where it is to be performed, enter into and form a part of it as if they were expressly referred to and incorporated in its terms. This principle embraces alike those which affect its validity, construction, discharge and enforcement. [Von Hoffman v. City of Quincy, 4 Wall. 535, 71 U.S. 535]

In another context, the same court said:

> Contracts, however expressed, cannot fetter the constitutional authority of the Congress. Contracts may create rights of property, but when contracts deal with a subject matter which lies within the control of the Congress, they have a congenital infirmity. Parties cannot remove their transactions from the reach of dominant constitutional power by making contracts about them. [Norman v. Baltimore and Ohio Railroad Company, 294 U.S. 240, 307-8]

Another court said it this way:

. . . all contracts are entered into subject to the proper exercise of a reserved police power of the state. [Zelinger v. Public Service Commission, 164 Colo 424, 435 P.2d 412, 416 (1967)]

This rule of "reserved police power" or "congenital infirmity" of contracts applies with equal force to federal and state constitutions, statutes and regulations as well as other governing and controlling rules, regulations, and ordinances whether state, county or city. There is a constitutional provision which provides that no state shall pass any law "impairing the obligation of contracts," and there have been many sophisticated and esoteric legal arguments about the apparent conflict between the two constitutional provisions. However, in modern times the "police power of the State" has clearly carried the day.

Any contract which contains an element that is illegal or prohibited, either by virtue of an express statute, the constitution, an ordinance, or as against public policy, presents serious legal problems for both parties. By way of example, suppose an owner of land and a contractor entered into a contract for the construction of a house. If the contractor does not have a proper license, cannot get a permit to build the house, or the zoning prohibits houses on the lot selected, there can be nothing but legal problems or lawsuits to follow. Or, suppose you enter into a contract with a person who is 17 years of age in a state where the legal age of majority is 18. You lose!

Suppose, further, that you entered into a contract with a "common carrier" trucking line regulated by the Interstate Commerce Commission to ship a truckload of goods from Phoenix, Arizona, to New York City for $1,000, whereas the regulatory tariff prescribes a rate of $3,000 for that item. The truck line can sue you and collect $3,000. That's the law! Your contract for $1,000 is no good! No matter what the contract says, the "reserved police power of the State" will prevail. It is essential that you avoid these entanglements by checking all available information before entering into a contract. It is as important to be properly prepared to enter into a contract, by knowing the subject matter of the contract and checking out the other party, as it is to know what to include in the written contract.

Changes in Contracts

The parties to a contract may modify it or waive their rights under it, and agree to new terms under a new or modified contract. The changes must be supported by consideration, as in any contract. It is always wise to have changes in writing. Always!

Legal Interpretation and Meaning of Terms

In determining what a paragraph, a sentence, a phrase, or a word in a contract means, the courts will generally apply the following principles: Effect must be given to the intention of the parties as gathered from the construction of the entire contract. The contract should receive a practical interpretation by the courts. Where a contract is understood by one of the parties in a certain sense and the other party knows that he so understands it, then the undertaking is to be taken in that sense, provided this can be done without making a new contract for the parties. The parties may, in the contract itself, define terms used in the contract.

Written matter in a contract controls printed matter where the two are inconsistent, but the courts will give effect to both if possible. A statute, regulation, tariff, or an ordinance prescribing subject matter regulations is considered a part of the contract. As we have already seen, a contract is subject to the applicable and governing laws regulating the subject matter of the contract. If the terms of the contract are clear and unambiguous, the court is bound to enforce the contract as it finds it. Since the terms of a plain, unambiguous contract cannot be varied or changed by the courts, it is important to understand the terms of a contract and to put any amendments or changes in writing.

Clauses in contracts providing for penalties or excessive liquidated damages for default or nonperformance are not favored by the courts, and are strictly construed. It is therefore suggested that you not rely too heavily on these provisions.

Breach of Contract: Lawsuits for Damages

Our discussions thus far have covered many of the general principles of law in the context of knowing what the law is, knowing what causes most lawsuits, and being able to prepare a contract which anticipates and alleviates most of the potential problems to the extent that it can reasonably be done. The time spent in working on your contract will reward you more than you will ever know. You can benefit from all the mistakes made by others and avoid the agony and burdens of an error or oversight.

If, however, you nevertheless enter into a contract and something does go wrong, you should know your rights and be prepared to handle the problem without further losses, confusion, and bewilderment. If you have a good contract, the lawsuit or dispute can generally be resolved without extensive litigation and acrimony. Typically, the most common breaches of contract consist of failure to pay money in accordance with the contract, and failure or refusal to perform in accordance with the contract. Some of the typical disputes that lead to these breaches of contract include such items as one party wanting more money; one party wanting more work, services or goods; partial or complete repudiation of the contract by one party; disagreements over quality of goods, work or materials; and the so-called excuses for nonperformance. And there are many more!

The typical kind of problem which generally results in a nasty lawsuit can be avoided most of the time if the parties know their own business and benefit from the past to the extent that provisions are made in the contract for the resolution of as many contingencies as the parties can reasonably anticipate. You can probably handle some lawsuits yourself, but if you need a lawyer, be sure not to delay too long before you get a good one.

What Damages Are Recoverable?

What happens when one party breaches a contract? If it does not cause the other party some damage or injury—nothing. Many people fail to live up to the promises they make, but seldom does it result in a lawsuit. First, lawsuits are very expensive for everybody; they are generally unpleasant for both sides; they take a lot of time; they can range from embarrassing to downright stultifying; and letting a jury decide a business dispute is like flipping a coin. But the main reason I advise you to avoid lawsuits for breach of contract has to do with the legal hassles over assessing the damages.

Just as it is difficult to decide if there *is* a contract, the rule of law on what a party is entitled to recover from another who breaches a contract is easier to state than it is to apply in actual cases. The famous English case of Hadley v. Baxendale (1854) gave a classic statement of the rule that has been followed today by most courts in this country. Every law student knows this case "word for word." The court announced the rule of law as follows:

> Where two parties have made a contract which one of them has broken, the damages which the other party ought to receive in respect of such breach of contract should be such as may fairly and reasonably be considered either arising naturally, i.e., according to the usual course of things, from such breach of contract itself, or such as may reasonably be supposed to have been in the contemplation of both parties, at the time they made the contract, as the probable result of the breach of it. [Hadley v. Baxendale, 9 Ex 341, 354; 156 Eng Rep 145, 151 (1854)]

Today, the typical jury instruction given by trial judges in these cases is to award "compensation for whatever loss or injury directly and proximately results from the defendant's wrongful act." The imagination of your lawyer in presenting the evidence and the quality of your evidence on the damage issue will be major factors in the outcome of your lawsuit.

Thus, your main problem in a breach of contract lawsuit is to produce evidence of all the damages you sustain and convince the jury you are entitled to all of them! A tough job: better to spend extra time in negotiating and preparing a good contract in your favor.

Discharge or Rescission of Contracts

Contracts may be discharged in many ways, including (1) performance, (2) breach, (3) impossibility of performance, (4) novation or change of agreement, (5) operation of law, or (6) rescission based on fraud, mistake, duress, or undue influence. Contracts may be rescinded by agreement of the parties, pursuant to statutes, or by the innocent party at his election, upon a number of grounds including default, excessive delays, repudiation, inability to perform, willful refusal to perform, fraud, misrepresentation or mutual mistake.

The right of a party to rescind a contract should be exercised promptly upon discovery of the facts from which the right to rescind arises. If the right is not exercised within a reasonable time, it may be waived. The effect of rescission is to extinguish the contract; it is annihilated so effectually that in the eyes of the law it has never had any existence.

In your discussions and negotiations leading up to contracts, you will have a great advantage if you know more about their essential elements and the laws governing them.

Novation: New Contracts

A novation of a contract is a mutual agreement among all parties to a contract to extinguish a valid existing contract by substituting a new contract. Any obligation that may be destroyed, including legacies, mortgages, negotiable instruments, and other contractual obligations, may be destroyed by novation. Novation may be accomplished by three methods.

1. A new obligee may be substituted for the original obligee with the intention on the part of all parties involved to discharge the original obligee from all duties under the original contract.

2. A new obligor may be substituted for the original obligor with the intention on the part of all the parties involved to release the original obligor of all obligations under the original contract.

3. The parties to the original contract may effect a novation by substituting an entirely new contract for the original contract, with the intention of completely extinguishing the original contract.

The effect of a novation that substitutes one party for another is to bind the substituted party to all the terms of the original contract to the same extent as the original party, so that the original party may not sue or be sued on the original obligation. A novation that substitutes one contract for another has the legal effect of completely extinguishing and terminating the original contract.

One of the problems created by the novation concept is that contracting parties frequently enter into written contracts and then continue to discuss the terms and conditions. These post-contractual verbal agreements about changes in the contract, may—or may not—be valid. This problem can be resolved by having a standard provision in a written contract to the effect that changes in the contract may be made only in writing.

4

Crimes, Criminals and Criminal Laws

What Is a Crime?

A *crime* is an offense against the state or sovereignty. It is an act committed, or omitted, in violation of a public law forbidding, or commanding it. A statute declaring something unlawful, but prescribing no penalty, does not create a crime. For example, in some states fornication and adultery are prohibited but carry no fines or penalties; seldom are these so-called offenses prosecuted, or convictions obtained. A crime is a wrong which the government claims is injurious to the public at large and punishes through a judicial proceeding in the name of the state. Although the same act may constitute both a crime and a tort, the crime is an offense against the public, while the tort is a private injury which may result in the injured party bringing a lawsuit in a civil court for the recovery of damages. This would constitute a tort action as discussed in Chapter 2.

Legal mental capacity to commit a crime is an essential requisite to criminal responsibility. Stated another way, an incompetent (insane) person is not capable of committing a crime.

At common law, a crime required two elements, (1) an act and (2) an evil intention. Under the common law, proof of criminal intent is a necessary element in the prosecution of every criminal case, except those offenses which are merely malum prohibitum. There are some crimes in which a wrongful intent is presumed solely from the commission of the act itself.

The law has long divided crimes into acts wrong in themselves, called acts *mala in se*, and acts which would not be wrong but for the facts that positive law forbids them, called acts *mala prohibita*. An act which is mala in se is one inherently wicked, one naturally evil, as adjudged by the sense of a civilized community; it is one involving illegality from the very nature of the transaction, upon principles of natural, moral, and public law, and one immoral in its nature and injurious in its consequences, without regard to the fact of its being noticed or punished by the law of the state.

A *criminal motive* is that which leads or tempts the mind to indulge in a criminal act; it is the moving power which impels to action for a definite result.

Malice is that state of mind which prompts the intentional doing of a wrongful act without legal justification or excuse.

Willful denotes an act which is intentional, or knowing, or voluntary, as distinguished from accidental.

Ordinarily one is not guilty of a crime unless he is aware of the existence of all those facts which make his conduct criminal, but there are some exceptions to this rule. For example, voluntary intoxication (getting drunk on whiskey) or narcosis (getting jacked up on drugs) is generally not a good defense to an unlawful act committed while "under the influence."

The word *criminal* denotes one who has committed a criminal offense, one who has been legally convicted of a crime, or one adjudged guilty of a crime. The rights of a citizen who is charged with a crime are discussed later. The word criminal used as an adjective denotes that which pertains to or is connected with the law of crimes, or the administration of penal justice, or which relates to or has the character of crime.

Criminal procedure is that set of rules administered by the criminal courts in the administration of the criminal system of justice.

Legal Rights of a U.S. Citizen

I have, from time to time, asserted that our federal government intrudes itself into our daily lives too much. But, by way of the "confessions of a mad lawyer," I must admit that the federal government has come through with flying colors when we consider the individual rights of citizens of the United States in criminal matters, as compared with other countries.

The U.S. Constitution, especially the Bill of Rights and the several amendments as interpreted by the Warren Court, a series of decisions by the U.S. Supreme Court from the late fifties to the early seventies, form the legal foundation for a wide range of protection of the citizen from criminal prosecution by the states or by the federal government. On balance, and from an historical and philosophical point of view, it is good. "Tyranny in the pursuit of justice isn't all bad."

The limitation of space does not permit a detailed discussion of each of the important criminal decisions of the U.S. Supreme Court, but we will discuss briefly the source of these decisions, and the rules developed. Rarely does one plan for future criminal proceedings in their personal lives, but it is very important for you to know your legal rights just in case you should be charged with a crime.

This is especially true if you are falsely charged, or if you get in a position where your lack of knowledge about your legal rights may result in your waiving them.

Don't be bashful in *demanding* your constitutional rights, including the Fifth Amendment. It's an absolute right you have. Here is only a partial list of your most fundamental rights:

1. Freedom of Speech and Freedom of the Press
2. Freedom of Assembly
3. Freedom of Religion

4. Right to Vote
5. Right to Hold Office
6. Right to Keep and Bear Arms
7. Right to Individual Privacy
8. Right to Full Enjoyment of your Property
9. Right to Equal Protection of the Laws
10. Right to Privilege Against Self-Incrimination
11. Right to Due Process of Law
12. Right to Habeas Corpus
13. Right Against Double Jeopardy
14. Right to a Jury Trial

All of these are very important rights; we all learned about them in school, but many American citizens soon forget about them. While they are all very important, I want to give you a brief review of how to apply these rules if you need them.

Your Legal Right to Represent Yourself in Court

You have a legal right to represent yourself in court, to be your own lawyer, if you wish to do so. You should be very careful, however, in exercising this right. Where substantial property rights or serious crimes are involved, you should always consider the services of a *good* lawyer; however, in small civil cases and minor criminal matters you may do better representing yourself. This is especially true in small cases where you frequently pay more in attorney's fees than the whole case is worth. The "free" lawyers provided by the state in criminal matters aren't all as good as Perry Mason, either! Many of them are among the large percentage of lawyers in this country who the Chief Justice of the United States has said are incompetent to handle trials. Just be careful to get a good, competent, experienced lawyer.

A federal statute, 28 U.S.C. 1654, provides:

> In all courts of the United States the parties may plead and conduct their own cases personally or by counsel as, by the rules of such courts, respectively, are permitted to manage and conduct causes therein.

The constitutions and statutes of many states have a similar provision.

As we have seen, you have a constitutional right to a lawyer in criminal cases, but what happens if the state provides you with a lawyer and you don't want him? Can the court force a lawyer upon you? No!

The U.S. Supreme Court recently held:

> The Sixth and Fourteenth Amendments of our Constitution guarantee that a person brought to trial in any state or federal court must be afforded the right to the assistance of counsel before he can be validly convicted and punished by imprisonment. This clear constitutional rule has emerged from a series of cases decided here over the last 50 years. The question before us now is whether a defendant in a state criminal trial has a constitutional right to proceed *without* counsel when he voluntarily and intelligently elects to do so. Stated another way, the question is whether a State may constitutionally hale a person into its criminal courts and there force a lawyer upon him, even when he insists that he wants to conduct his own defense.

It is not an easy question, but we have concluded that a State may not constitutionally do so. [Faretta v. California, 422 U.S. 806 (1975)]

With all their defects, most courts in this country, both criminal and civil, are far superior to those of most countries except, perhaps, England and Canada. And with all the criticism of lawyers, many lawyers in this country are superior in their dedication to service even though they have to charge high fees. You can improve your position greatly if you realize that all lawyers aren't qualified to handle *all* kinds of cases, and approach the selection of a lawyer with care and with an investigative attitude. You can save on legal fees by doing some legal research yourself; it's not all that complicated.

What to Do If You Get Arrested

If you should ever be arrested and charged with a crime, it will be too late then to try to look at some legal manual to discover your rights and to learn what you should do to protect your interests. You should review these steps carefully and understand all your rights because they could be of critical importance in the event you ever have the full force and power of the state on your case.

We have all heard about the legal rights of Americans who are accused of a crime, for example, the Miranda rights, the Fifth Amendment rights, and others. But how do we apply these legal principles in practice once we are arrested? Generally, when one is arrested, one of the most important activities that will follow is a search for evidence. As a general rule, one charged with a serious crime should not give any evidence to the cops without competent legal advice from a lawyer who knows enough about the case to form an intelligent judgment. Every person in the United States who is accused of a crime has a right to an attorney, even if he cannot afford one, and every person taken into custody must be notified of his right to remain silent and of his right to have an attorney present throughout the process of his arraignment, preliminary hearing, and trial.

As a citizen of the United States, one has the following rights among others:

1. In making an arrest, the police must inform the accused of his rights and give him an opportunity to phone a relative, friend or lawyer.

2. The accused has the right to a lawyer's services from the moment of arrest, and need not say anything until he consults with his lawyer.

3. He has a right to know the charges against him.

4. He has a right to a reasonably prompt hearing before a magistrate.

5. If held for trial, the accused has a right to have reasonable bail set as security for his release, except for certain major crimes or at the discretion of the court.

6. He has a right to a reasonably prompt jury trial.

7. He has a right to confront and cross-examine his accusers and to call witnesses on his own behalf.

8. He cannot be tried twice for the same offense.

9. If he is convicted, he cannot be subjected to cruel and unusual punishment.

An accused may knowingly waive these rights, but it is foolish to waive them, especially those of such fundamental importance to citizens. With the full force (and financing) of the state or federal government on the other side, an accused will need all the help he can get.

The most important thing for an accused to remember is (1) don't talk and (2) get a good lawyer.

Your Lawyer

When you do obtain the services of an attorney, you should be prepared to give him pertinent information that will help in your defense. Generally the things you should be prepared to give your attorney include the following:

1. Facts of the case, including details of the alleged crime.
2. Names and addresses of persons who might be witnesses to the facts of the crime; that is, possible witnesses to disprove the crime.
3. Prior criminal record, if any.
4. Employment record.
5. Persons who could be used as character witnesses.
6. Persons who could testify to an alibi, if applicable.

55

7. Relatives and friends who could assist in obtaining bail.
8. Personal business which must be completed during period you are in jail awaiting the posting of bail.
9. Details of the arrest.

Preliminary Hearings

The accused is generally entitled to have a preliminary hearing on any charges against him within a reasonable time after arrest. At this hearing, the state is required to establish that a crime was committed and that there is reasonable and proper cause to believe that the accused committed the crime charged. It is not necessary for the state to prove its accusations beyond reasonable doubt at this time.

At the preliminary hearing the defense attorney has the right to cross examine the witnesses called by the state, although he has no obligation to call witnesses on the defendant's case. In some cases, however, the attorney for the accused may want to call witnesses on his case in order to preserve testimony of witnesses who may leave the jurisdiction or die, or otherwise establish testimony for use later. In some states the defense of insanity and alibi should be raised at the preliminary hearing if they are to be relied on by the defendant. If a confession or admission of the defendant is utilized by the prosecution and the defendant contends that it was extracted by force, the validity and propriety of the confession should be raised at the earliest possible time. Where the defendant fails to raise these issues at the earliest possible time, that failure may subsequently be used against him in the determination of the propriety of the confession.

At the preliminary hearing or subsequently at the arraignment, the defendant will have an opportunity to object to any illegal search or seizure. If the defendant's premises have been searched in violation of his constitutional rights or his person has been searched, except as an incident to an otherwise legal arrest, the evidence thus obtained may not be admissible. In some states if the defendant was aware of the illegal search, he must raise the issue prior to trial or it may be waived.

The validity of the arrest may also be determined at the preliminary hearing, if it is at issue. In most states, the powers of the peace officer or a citizen to make an arrest are spelled out by statute. The rules relating to the validity of an arrest may vary depending on the crime charged.

Grand Jury

If the defendant is accused of a felony, the case will generally be submitted to a grand jury. The grand jury is required to inquire into crimes and make accusations in accordance with the law.

To find an indictment, the grand jury must rely on legal evidence, that is, sworn testimony, depositions and documentary proof. The evidence presented need only make out a prima facie case, that is, every element of the crime must be established. Generally, the crime will be established before the grand jury in broad terms, leaving details to be established later at the trial.

In some cases the defendant may volunteer to appear before the grand jury, but he will not have a right to appear before a grand jury unless it is specifically provided by statute. Where the defendant appears before the grand jury, it is usually without counsel, and after the defendant has agreed to waive immunity.

In most states the grand jury is not limited to investigating and returning indictments concerning defendants already in custody. In its discretion, the grand jury can also undertake broad investigations.

Generally the defendant in a criminal case may have the right to refuse to testify before a grand jury if he has been accused of a crime or if the testimony would tend to incriminate him. Where the defendant does not have the right to refuse to testify, he will have the right to refuse to answer specific questions in the event that his answer would incriminate him. Although the court must be the final judge of whether a question will incriminate the defendant, lack of knowledge generally forces the court to rely upon the defendant for the determination. It would not be proper to ask a defendant why he was invoking the privilege afforded by the Fifth Amendment to the U.S. Constitution.

An accused will not be permitted to avail himself of his constitutional right against self-incrimination where he has been granted immunity. In many jurisdictions the immunity will only be applicable to prosecutions in that jurisdiction. Similarly, a defendant will not be excused from answering questions if the answer would tend to incriminate him with respect to a crime for which the statute of limitations has run or if the answer would merely tend to subject the defendant to civil liability.

The grand jury will either render an indictment against the defendant or refuse to render an indictment. Where the grand jury renders the indictment, the defendant will be arraigned.

Arraignment

The arraignment to the charge or arraignment to the indictment gives the defendant an opportunity to hear the indictment rendered by the grand jury. The reading of the indictment may be dispensed with where the defendant has been provided with a copy prior to the arraignment.

Sometimes, prior to the arraignment, the defendant's attorney may have had preliminary discussions with the prosecutor's office concerning the charge and the pleas which the defendant will enter. In settling a criminal case, the defendant may agree to plead guilty to a lesser charge, thereby eliminating the need for trial. A great majority of criminal cases are settled before trial. In many cases, however, a criminal case will be more difficult to settle than a civil case because of the influence of intensive public attention, political pressures, or the defendant's refusal to plead guilty to any charge. Where a plea is being worked out, it may be possible to obtain a commitment from the judge as to the sentence which will be imposed. Where the judge will not commit himself in advance, it may be necessary to rely on experience with a particular judge in sentencing, or the statutory maximum and minimum sentence for the crime charged. Where sentencing has been discussed with the court prior to entering pleas for several crimes, counsel should determine whether the sentences to be imposed by the court will run concurrently or consecutively.

Motions

Although your attorney will be handling most of the legal proceedings, it is important for you to know and understand these proceedings. Generally motions during the preliminary proceedings include the following: (1) bill of particulars; (2) motions to inspect the minutes of the grand jury; (3) motions to quash, dismiss or set aside the indictment; and (4) a demurrer.

Before trial most defendants will exhaust all plea bargaining, a practice in most areas of the nation. Prosecuting attorneys are notoriously overworked (they say), and it is frequently common practice for defendants to be able to get off with a lesser charge, thereby avoiding a trial.

Every defendant is entitled to a fair trial, by jury in most cases, and he may appeal any verdict or judgment entered against him.

Kinds of Crimes

Crimes are generally classified as felony or misdemeanor. Minor violations (like traffic fines) are punishable offenses, but are not generally considered to be in the classification of a crime, in the sense that you have a criminal record.

A *felony* is an offense that is punishable by death or by imprisonment in a state or federal prison. You will sometimes see these felonies referred to as capital crimes or infamous crimes. These terms, however, have little legal significance today because various crimes are specifically defined in the criminal statutes. All other crimes, which carry less severe penalties, are *misdemeanors*. The so-called *violations* are punished less severely than crimes. The distinction between felonies and misdemeanors, on the one hand, and violations, on the other, is really the difference in the severity of punishment which is provided for the crime or offense in the law defining it. Typical felonies we hear about are murder, rape, larceny, arson, burglary and treason.

Another important difference between felonies and misdemeanors and all other lower offenses lies in your right to trial by jury: if you are suspected of having committed a felony or a more serious misdemeanor, you are brought before a grand jury, indicted, arraigned, given a chance to plead in any one of several ways (guilty, not guilty, nole contendre), and offered a jury trial. But if your offense is relatively minor, a less serious misdemeanor a violation, you may be arraigned or brought into court at the motion of the local prosecuting attorney and given a chance to plead. You may or may not have an absolute right to trial by jury. More about this later.

Misdemeanors are offenses which, because they are regarded as less dangerous to society, less evil in themselves, carry a less severe penalty than felonies. Therefore, your legal rights and constitutional protections are not as great in misdemeanors and violations as they are for more serious charges.

Principals, Accessories and Accomplices

If you commit a crime you are, of course, the principal in the criminal proceedings. But, there's more. Those who participate in the commission of a crime are also subject to the criminal process.

An *accessory* is one who contributes to or aids in the commission of a crime. It is one who, without being present at the commission of a felonious offense, becomes guilty of such offense, not as a chief actor but as a partici-

pator, as by command, advice, instigation, or conceal-
ment, either before or after the fact or commission.

An *accessory before the fact* is one who, being absent
at the time a crime is committed, yet assists, procures,
counsels, incites, induces, encourages, engages, or com-
mands another to commit it. An *accessory during the fact*
is one who stands by without interfering or giving such
help as may be in his power to prevent the commission of
a criminal offense.

An *accessory after the fact* is one who, having full
knowledge that a crime has been committed, conceals it
from the magistrate and harbors, assists, or protects the
person charged with, or convicted of, a crime. All persons
who, after the commission of any felony, conceal or aid
the offender, with knowledge that he has committed a
felony, and with intent that he may avoid or escape from
arrest, trial, conviction or punishment, are accessories.

Conspiracy

This is defined as a combination or confederacy between two or more persons formed for the purpose of
committing, by their joint efforts, some unlawful or criminal act, or some act which is innocent in itself, but
becomes unlawful when done by the concerted action of
the conspirators, or for the purpose of using criminal or
unlawful means to the commission of an act not in itself
unlawful. The essence of a conspiracy, according to the
United States Supreme Court, is an agreement, together

with an overt act, to do an unlawful act, or to do a lawful act in an unlawful manner. The mere knowledge, acquiescence, approval or attempt on the part of one to perpetrate an illegal act is insufficient. It is a partnership in crime.

Sedition

Sedition may be defined as an active movement tending towards treason, but lacking an overt act. It consists of attempts made by meetings or speeches, or by publications, to disturb the tranquillity of the state or nation. The difference between sedition and treason is that although the ultimate object of sedition is a violation of the public peace, or at least such a course of measures as evidently engenders it, yet it does not aim at direct and open violence against the laws or the subversion of the constitution. Sedition involves actively urging the overthrow of the state, not simply discussing revolution as a philosophical matter. It comes close to the borders of freedom of speech and as a result, there have been few prosecutions for the crime of sedition in modern times.

Contempt

In its broadest sense, contempt is a willful disregard or disobedience of a public authority. This public authority may be a legislative body (Congress), administrative agencies, courts of law, or others. Generally, the term is thought of as "contempt of court," which is an act that is calculated to embarrass, hinder, or obstruct the court in the administration of justice, or which is calculated to lessen its authority or its dignity.

Contempts are of two kinds, direct and constructive. Direct contempt is one that is committed in the immediate view and presence of the court (such as insulting language or acts of violence) or so near the presence of the court as to obstruct or interrupt the due and orderly course of the proceedings. These, also called criminal contempts, are punishable summarily. Summarily means "quick and dirty"; the judge can send you *straight* to jail.

Constructive contempts are those which arise from matters not occurring in or near the presence of the court, but which tend to obstruct or defeat the administration of justice, and the term is chiefly used with reference to the failure or refusal of a party to obey a lawful order, injunction, or decree of the court placing upon him a duty of action or forebearance.

Contempt of court is further classified as civil or criminal. *Civil contempts* are those which consist in the failure to do something which the party is ordered by the court to do for the benefit or advantage of another party to the proceedings before the court, while *criminal contempts* are acts done in disrespect of the court or its process or which obstruct the administration of justice or tend to bring the court into disrespect.

Contempt of Congress is that which obstructs or tends to obstruct the due course of proceedings of either house, or grossly reflects on the character of a member of either house, or imputes to him what it would be libel to impute to an ordinary person.

Perjury

This, in criminal law, is the willful assertion as a matter of fact, opinion, belief, or knowledge, made by a witness in a judicial proceeding as part of his evidence, either upon oath or in any form allowed by law to be substituted for an oath, whether such evidence is given in open court, or in an affidavit, or otherwise, such assertion being material to the issue or point of inquiry and known to such witness to be false. Perjury, at common law, was the taking of a willful false oath by one who, being lawfully sworn by a competent court to depose the truth in any judicial proceedings, swore absolutely and falsely in a matter material to the point in issue, whether he believed it or not. While at common law it was confined to judicial proceedings, by statute in many states perjury has been extended to willful false swearing in many different kinds of affidavits and depositions, such as those required to be made in tax returns, pension proceedings, transactions with administrative agencies, and various other non-judicial proceedings.

In common parlance it is telling a lie under oath.

Blackmail

The crime of blackmail is the extortion of money by threats of overtures towards criminal prosecution or the destruction of a person's reputation or social standing. In common usage, the term is equivalent to, and synonymous with, extortion. It is the exaction of money, either for the performance of a duty, the prevention of an injury, or the exercise of an influence. It supposes the service to be unlawful, and the payment involuntary. Blackmail is sometimes exerted by threats, or by operating upon the fears or the credulity, or by promises to conceal, or offers to expose, the weaknesses, the follies, or the crimes of the victim.

Extortion

Extortion is the unlawful obtaining of money from another. It is the corrupt demanding or receiving by a person in office of a fee for services which should be performed without charge; or, where compensation is permissible, of a larger fee than the law justifies, or a fee not due; the exaction of money by reason of oppressive conditions or circumstances; obtaining of property from another, with his consent, induced by wrongful use of force or fear, or under color of official right. The term signifies an oppression under the color of right, and in a strict or technical sense signifies unlawful taking by any officer, under color of office, of any money or thing of value not due him, more than is due, or before it is due.

Forgery

This constitutes the false making or material altering, with intent to defraud, of any writing which, if genuine, might appear to be of legal efficacy or the foundation of a legal liability. It is the fraudulent making and alteration of a writing to the prejudice of another person's right; or a false making, a making malo animo (with an evil mind; with a bad purpose or wrongful intention, with malice) of any instrument, for the purpose of fraud or deceit. It is also the thing itself, so falsely made, imitated or forged, especially a forged writing. A forged signature is sometimes called a "forgery."

Bribery

Bribery is the offering, giving, receiving, or soliciting of anything of value to influence action as official or in discharge of legal or public duty; the corrupt tendering or receiving of a price for official action. Originally the offense applied only to corrupt giving to judges. Then it was broadened to cover bribes to all public officials, and in recent years it has been extended to include giving to and receiving from people generally for illicit purposes, such as paying money to voters to vote a certain way or to an athlete to throw a game. By law, in most states, bribery is a felony.

Obstruction of Justice

The Watergate Seven made this crime famous! It is the act by which one or more persons attempt to prevent, or do prevent, the execution of lawful process. The term applies also to obstructing the administration of justice in any way, as by hindering witnesses from appearing, or in having witnesses fail to tell the truth. It includes any impeding or obstructing of those who seek justice in a court, or those who have duties or powers of administering justice in the courts.

Disturbing the Peace

Interruption of the peace, quiet, and good order of a neighborhood or community, particularly by unnecessary and distracting noises. It includes any act that is committed without lawful justification which unreasonably disturbs the public peace or tends strongly to create or encourage disturbance. It is sometimes called disorderly conduct. It is a catchall phrase to include a bunch of wrongful acts; when the cop can't think of a more specific charge to make against you, he can almost always charge you with "disturbing the peace."

Bigamy

The criminal offense of willfully and knowingly contracting a second marriage (or going through the form of a second marriage) while the first marriage, to the knowledge of the offender, is still undissolved. It is the state of a man who has two wives, or a woman who has two husbands, living at the same time.

Adultery

The voluntary sexual intercourse of a married person with a person other than his or her husband or wife. Fornication is sexual intercourse between two pesons not married to each other. The penalties, under the statutes of most states where adultery is a violation, vary greatly and the act is seldom prosecuted as a crime. In some states adultery is not a crime; in other states the statutes making it criminal have been declared unconstitutional by the courts. Rarely are cases involving adultery or fornication brought to court.

Incest

The sexual intercourse or cohabitation between a man and woman who are related to each other within the degrees wherein marriage is prohibited by law. The rules of law on marriage may vary from state to state.

Crimes Against the Person and Real Property

Homicide

The killing of one human being by the act, procurement, or omission of another. This term includes every mode by which the life of another person is taken by a slayer. It does not necessarily import a crime, since one's act in taking another's life may be excusable or justifiable. The common law divides homicide into murder, manslaughter, excusable homicide, and justifiable homicide.

As defined by statutes in most states, felonious homicide is either *murder,* in some one of the degrees, as defined by the statutes, or *manslaughter,* depending upon the presence or absence of malice, express or implied, and of premeditation and deliberation, or upon the fact that the homicide was committed by the slayer during the perpetration of another felony.

The word murder is a technical word, or a "term of art" which has acquired a peculiar meaning in the law generally, and in many states has been defined by statute. The grade or degree of homicide in any particular case depends on the intent, purpose, or design of the slayer. The element which distinguishes murder from manslaughter, or which marks the boundary between the two grades of homicide, is malice.

Generally, most states define the grades of homicide as follows:

1. First Degree (Murder One!): The unlawful killing of a human being with malice aforethought. Deliberation or premeditation—a design to take life—is the key factor.

2. Second Degree Murder: Where an unlawful killing is shown and the evidence does not disclose express malice or a state of facts which would justify or excuse the homicide or reduce it to manslaughter, the slayer is guilty of murder in the second degree. Some statutes define second degree murder as a killing perpetuated by any act imminently dangerous to others and evincing a depraved mind regardless of human life, although without any premeditation or design to effect the death of any particular individual.

3. Manslaughter: A homicide which is not first or second degree and not justifiable nor excused in law; an unlawful killing of a human being done without malice

express or implied, either in a sudden quarrel or unintentionally while in the commission of an unlawful act.

Motive is the impulse or purpose which leads or moves the mind to perpetuate a criminal act, whether it is murder or some other crime. Motive is the moving cause which induces action, and has wholly to do with desire; *intent* is the purpose of design with which an act is done and involves the will of the person.

Malice is the intentional doing of a wrongful act without just cause or excuse, with an intent to inflict an injury or under circumstances that the law will imply an evil intent.

Malice aforethought means a predetermination to commit an act without legal justification or excuse.

In the definition of murder, malice aforethought exists where the person doing the act which causes death has an intention to cause death or grievous bodily harm to any person, whether the person is actually killed or not, or to commit any felony whatever, or has the knowledge that the act will probably cause the death of or grievous bodily harm to some person, although he does not desire it, or even wishes that it may not be caused.

The words malice aforethought long ago acquired in law a settled meaning, somewhat different from the popular one. In their legal sense they do not import an actual intention to kill the deceased. The idea is not spite or malevolence to the deceased in particular, but evil design in general, the dictate of a wicked, depraved, and malignant heart; not premeditated personal hatred or revenge towards the person killed, but that kind of unlawful purpose which, if persevered in, must produce mischief.

Corpus delecti means the body of the offense (not necessarily the physical body of a person), the substance of the crime. As applied to homicide cases it has at least two component elements, (1) the fact of death; and (2) the criminal agency of another person as the cause of it.

In some states, the identity of the slain person is a third element, but other courts reject this view. One court has stated that the evidence to establish the corpus delecti must show that the life of a human being has been taken, which question involves the subordinate inquiry as to the identity of the person charged to have been killed.

Rape

The unlawful carnal knowledge of a woman by a man forcibly and against her will. If she consents to the sexual intercourse, although her consent may be reluctantly given, and although there may be some force used to obtain her consent, the offense is not rape. Modern statutes often materially change the common law definition and create an offense commonly known as *statutory rape,* where the offense consists in having sexual intercourse with a female under statutory age, whether or not the female consents.

73

Assault and Battery

An *assault* is an intentional, unlawful offer of corporal injury to another by force, or force unlawfully directed toward the person of another, under such circumstances coupled with apparent present ability to execute the attempt, if not prevented. A *battery* is the unlawful beating, or other wrongful physical violence or constraint, inflicted on a human being without his consent. It is the willful and unlawful use of force or violence upon the person of another. An assault and battery is a tort which may also be a crime: this means that one charged with assault and battery may get sued for damages and he may also go to jail.

Aggravated assault is assault with intent to murder, rob, rape or do serious bodily harm.

Arson

Arson, at common law, meant the malicious burning of the house or outhouse of another. In most states, this crime is divided into arson in the first, second, and the third degrees. The *first degree* includes the burning of an inhabited dwelling house in the nighttime; *second degree*, the burning (at night) of a building other than a dwelling house, but so situated with reference to a dwelling house as to endanger it; and the *third degree*, the burning of any building or structure not the subject of arson in the first or second degree, or the burning of property, with intent to defraud or prejudice an insurer thereof. Each state statute must be reviewed to determine the law of any specific state.

Burglary

At common law, burglary was the breaking and entering, in the nighttime, of the dwelling or mansion house of another, with intent to commit a felony therein. Common law burglary involves circumstances, each of which is an essential element of the crime and must be proved. These elements are: (1) a breaking; (2) an entry; (3) in the nighttime; (4) in a mansion house or dwelling house; and (5) with intent to commit a felony in the dwelling or mansion house.

All states have statutory definitions similar to the common law rules, but in many instances the statutes are more liberal and significantly broader than the common law rules.

Crimes Involving Personal Property

Larceny

Larceny is the felonious taking and carrying away of someone else's personal property, without his consent, with the intention of permanently depriving him of its use or possession. The exact definition will vary from state to state; however, courts have said it is the fraudulent taking and carrying away of a thing without claim or right, with intention of converting it to the use other than that of the owner, without his consent. It is the obtaining

75

of possession of property by fraud, trick or device with preconceived design or intent to appropriate, convert or steal it. Generally, one who unlawfully takes another's personal property, not intending to steal, and afterwards converts it, intending to steal, is guilty of larceny. Every act of a thief in the removal of personal property is in itself a complete larceny.

There are several varieties of larceny including compound larceny, constructive larceny, grand larceny, larceny by bailee, larceny from the person, mixed larceny, petit larceny, simple larceny, and others.

Robbery

Robbery is the felonious taking of personal property in the possession of another, from his person or immediate presence, and against his will, accomplished by means of force or fear. In a robbery a person, either with violence or with threats of injury, and putting the person robbed in fear, takes and carries away a thing which is on the body, or in the immediate presence of the person from whom it is taken, under such circumstances that, in the absence of violence or threats, the act committed would be a theft. Generally speaking, the elements of robbery are the taking of personal property or money from the person or presence of another by actual or constructive force without his consent and with animus furandi, or intent to steal. Robbery is compound larceny, composed of the crime of larceny from the person with the aggravation of force, actual or constructive, used in the taking. The exact wording of each state statute should be consulted to get the precise definition in each state.

Receiving Stolen Property

This term, or *receiving stolen goods*, is the short name usually given to the offense of receiving any property with the knowledge that it has been feloniously, or unlawfully stolen, taken, extorted, obtained, embezzled, or disposed of. Most state statutes require that the offense has several elements: (1) the accused must actually have received the property; (2) it must have been stolen and remain stolen at the time of its receipt; (3) the receiver must have known that the property was stolen; and (4) he must have received it with criminal intent, that is, intent to prevent the owner from getting it back.

Knowledge by the receiver that the property is stolen may be implied by the courts from the circumstances of the case. If property is in fact stolen, the receiver accepts it "with knowledge" if (1) he knows it was stolen, (2) he believes it was stolen, or (3) his suspicions are aroused and he does not check further for fear that he will discover it was stolen.

Embezzlement

The fraudulent appropriation to his own use or benefit of property or money intrusted to him by another, by a clerk, agent, trustee, public officer, or other person acting in a fiduciary character. Embezzlement is the fraudulent appropriation of property by a person to whom it has been intrusted, or to whose hands it has lawfully come. Embezzlement was not an offense at common law, but was created by statute. The term *embezzle* includes in its meaning appropriation to one's own use, and therefore the use of the single word embezzle in the indictment or information, contains within itself the charge that the defendant appropriated the money or property to his own use. Essentially it is common law larceny extended by statute to cover cases where the stolen property comes originally into the possession of the defendant without a trespass. Embezzlement is a species of larceny, and the term is applicable to cases of furtive and fraudulent appropriation by clerks, servants, or carriers of property coming into their possession by virtue of their employment.

Embezzlement is distinguished from larceny in that the property taken is not at the time in the actual or legal possession of the owner. In embezzlement the original taking of the property is lawful or with the consent of the owner; in larceny the felonious intent must have existed at the time of the taking.

Theft

This is just another name for larceny. It is the fraudulent taking of corporeal personal property belonging to another, from his possession, or from the possession of some person holding the same for him, without his consent, with intent to deprive the owner of the value of the property, and to appropriate it to the use or benefit of the person taking it. In general parlance the term theft has frequently been used to include such terms as swindling and embezzlement. Thus, anyone who "takes" the property of another by whatever means is referred to as a "thief."

Vandalism

Originally this word meant the willful or ignorant destruction of artistic or literary treasures; hostility to or contempt for what is beautiful or venerable. In modern usage it is generally used to describe any destruction of property without just cause.

Economic or White Collar Crimes

Economic crime can be defined simply as lying, cheating, and stealing. It is, at times, highly sophisticated and incredibly complex and it is, at times, brutally simple both in plan and in execution.

Economic crime is chameleon-like; it waffles in and out of all economic activities; its variations are infinite. It feeds on avarice, gullibility and innocence; deceit is its hallmark and monetary gain is its motive.

These criminals are very good planners; some are master planners; all have a wicked heart. Economic crime plans can be intricate and artful and its best practitioners are also journeymen in the art of improvisation. It has

79

been suggested that the "con artist" has an unnatural compulsion or obsession (similar to that of a sex pervert) to inflict hurt upon other people and upon society at large. He is "getting even" for something! Indeed, I have known crooks who had all the talents and qualifications to be very successful in business or in the professions, but who would invariably choose to be cheats, liars, deceitful crooks.

Economic criminals use the law, as they use business custom and practice, to their advantage. They are master salesmen, and they are usually likeable folks. At times the best schemes may be buried deep within an avalanche of ledgers, annual reports and registration statements. These paper trails are difficult to find, and even more difficult to follow.

Economic criminals are frequently respectable citizens, and they are clever in covering their schemes and manipulations beneath a mantle of respectability. They skillfully exploit the talents of the professions, arts and sciences to lend credence and substance to their schemes.

These people are often highly motivated and spend an enormous amount of energy pursuing their goals: defrauding. They are so clever in the "cover up" that they are frequently the admired and church-going acquaintances of honest citizens!

They are, from time to time, glamorous and charming "con" artists. More frequently, however, they blend in with the general run of society and are neither more nor less conspicuous than those around them.

Economic criminals are imaginative opportunists, quick to see advantage and fast in exploiting that advantage. They are mobile and they have learned to use technology for their gain. They are all these things, but in the final analysis, they are criminals—criminals so schooled in lying, cheating, and stealing that they make a "profession" out of it.

Their combined exploits cheat the taxpayers and the tax collectors alike of an estimated $40 billion annually, according to a report of the U.S. Chamber of Commerce. The gross estimate relates only to the initial direct cost to society. It does not include secondary losses, which may well exceed the $40 billion loss per year.

While economic criminals are selective in choosing victims, almost no group escapes their attention. Young and old, black and white, laborers and managers, business and industry—all get taken by the con artists. The government and all its agencies, in its roles as social caretaker and general program manager, is a target of opportunity for the economic criminals. The criminal will lie, cheat or steal from anybody, but the most sought after groups are (1) the soon-to-retire worker for those who peddle investment schemes; (2) the ambitious, undereducated striver who is a target for business opportunity schemes; (3) people who are not mechanically inclined and thus are targets for auto repair, appliance repair and home improvement frauds; (4) middle income citizens, targets for "vacation" and "resort" property frauds, the swamplands of Florida, or the rock and sand dunes of Arizona; (5) senior citizens who are targets for retirement community and nursing home frauds and various health and welfare frauds; (6) brokerage houses, corporations and financial institutions that are targets for computer assisted theft schemes. Finally, governments—at all levels—are targets for bid-rigging frauds, procurement frauds and a host of contractual schemes.

The effects of economic crime are self-multiplying. They almost always reach beyond the original victim and carry their own "ripple effect" across society at large. For example, let's consider the economic criminal who succeeds, with the aid of inside confederates, in obtaining a major construction contract on a public works project. First, he arranges a kickback to his governmental confederates in order to get the contract. The kickback money, which is generally a considerable sum, would normally go to procure skilled laborers and quality materials. Assuming the economic criminal has "arranged" his winning bid because he has lied about the quality of materials to be employed, there will ultimately arise the question of public safety, issues of municipal liability, issues of insurance liability and many other liabilities resulting from the poor quality of materials and work. Finally, assume that the public works project has been completed and substantial defects become apparent. Performance bonds or other secured guarantees may be defaulted; injuries may result; and repairs, at great additional cost, may be required. The contractor—the crook—generally leaves town with the money and his inside confederates remain invisible. Lawsuits follow at great expense and to little avail. Insurance companies, bonding agencies and, ultimately, the public treasury are left holding the bag. The economic criminals have the money and the public has the resulting white elephant. What has really happened?

First, in restraint of trade, two or more individuals have organized to deprive government and the public of the right to a quality contract arrived at through legitimate, arms-length competitive bidding. Second, bribes have been paid by the contractors to "buy" the contract and governmental process has been corrupted. Next, theft has occurred (most assuredly grand theft) by the use of materials below standard grades and specifications called for by the contract. To get away with this aspect of the scheme, building inspectors would have to be bought and the list of specific charges and offenses would continue for a long, long time. The original bribe to secure the cooperation of an insider was just a drop in the bucket. When the economic criminal's bucket is finally emptied, its ripples are felt by many. Every ripple was caused by lying, cheating, and stealing, and we all lose.

Moreover, the ripple effects of economic crime are not limited solely to those offenses involving major multi-million dollar contracts. The retiree who is defrauded of his life savings ultimately becomes a ward of the public treasury, and the small business driven to bankruptcy by the economic offenders casts it workers onto the welfare and unemployment rolls. Again, the personal enrichment of the economic criminal is but a small part of the total cost to society; and somewhere, somehow, the "need" felt by the crook to lash out and hurt has perhaps been satisfied in a warped, sick way.

The losses from economic crime and the damage done to individuals, to companies and to government alike are massive in scope. You have probably heard or read about some of these schemes. If you haven't been taken yet, watch out. Here are a list of some of the most prevalent schemes currently making the rounds:

1. Advance Fee Schemes
2. Pyramid Schemes
3. Chain Referral Schemes
4. Ponzi Schemes
5. Business Opportunity Schemes
6. Planned Bankruptcy Schemes
7. Service and Repair Schemes
8. Land Schemes
9. Home Improvement, Debt Counseling and Mortgage Loan Schemes

10. Home Solicitation Schemes

11. Personal Improvement Schemes

12. Frauds against Government Programs

13. Official Corruption

14. Bid Rigging

15. Commercial Bribery

16. Insurance Fraud

17. Computer Related Frauds

18. Credit Card Frauds

19. Charity Frauds

20. Check Kiting

In modern criminology, each crime is now almost exclusively defined with precision in the state or federal statutes. The definitions given here are not intended to reflect any particular statutory definition of specific crimes in any jurisdiction, but are limited to the generally accepted common law and general descriptions and definitions. In any specific case you must obtain a copy of the applicable statute to get the exact definition and punishment for a specific crime.

As you probably know, there are a wide range of other activities that may be classified by various statutes as crimes or violations.

5

Business Law

Business law includes the rules that govern almost every activity of all citizens, whether those activities are thought of as personal, business, or even criminal. When you buy a car or a dishwasher you may become involved in a number of business law rules. If you violate a statute governing your corporation or partnership, you are involved in business law, and if you have a dispute in a divorce proceeding about income taxes or a division of property, you may be engaged in business law rules.

Indeed business law encompasses so many aspects of our daily lives that it cannot be adequately covered in the limited space here. However, we will discuss some of the areas of business law that you are most likely to find important to you in terms of your operating a going business. Other books in the Citizens Law Library cover some of the topics in more detail.

Selection of Business Entity
Starting a new business is a very complex undertaking for most people, so before you get started on a new

business venture, you should learn all you can about the kind of business entity that is best for you. There are many factors that you must consider, the most significant of which are the following:

1. Liability exposure;
2. Tax costs and considerations;
3. Organizational expenses and costs;
4. Centralization of management;
5. Advantages of raising capital through issuance of stock;
6. Ability to attract and keep key personnel through various fringe benefits or participational stockholders; and
7. The practical convenience of the various forms in which a business might be conducted.

As the risk of potential personal liability increases, whether from the nature of the business or from the extent of your assets, the value of eliminating personal liability increases and the advantage of the corporate form increases. The small expenses involved in setting up a corporation are relatively insignificant when compared with other factors. Unless you fall into the "foreign corporation" trap, in which you expose yourself to unnecessary personal liabilities, penalties and costs, you can accomplish almost all business activities through incorporating in your own state.

Forms of Business Entities

The three most common forms of business organization are: individual proprietorships, partnerships, and corporation.

Other forms of business organization include limited partnerships, joint ventures, trusts, combination of partnerships and corporations, multiple corporations, incorporate but keeping certain assets out of the corporation, corporation electing not to pay corporate tax, Sub Chapter S elections, and others.

Individual Proprietorship

The single proprietorship is usually defined as a business which is owned and operated by one person. To establish a single proprietorship, you need only obtain whatever licenses are required and begin operations. Therefore, it is the most widely used form of small business organization.

There are few formalities or legal restrictions associated with establishing a single proprietorship. It needs little or no governmental approval and is usually less expensive than a partnership or corporation. The proprietor is not required to share profits with anyone, but he is usually required to finance the entire operation of the business, and therefore stands to lose more if the business does not succeed. There are no co-owners or partners to consult. Management is able to respond quickly to business needs in the form of day-to-day management decisions as governed by various laws and common sense. The business in this form is relatively free from government control and special taxation.

There are some disadvantages to the individual proprietorship. There is unlimited liability in that the individual is responsible for the full amount of business debt, which may extend to all the proprietor's assets, including his house and car. Additional problems of liability, such as physical loss or personal injury, may be lessened by obtaining proper insurance coverage. The enterprise may be crippled or terminated upon the illness or death of the owner. There is generally less capital available than other types of business organization, and there may be difficulty in obtaining long-term financing. In some instances it may be wise for a business owner to start a business operation as an individual proprietor and later form other business entities as the business grows and potential liabilities increase.

The Corporation

A corporation has been defined by the United States Supreme Court as "an artificial being, invisible, intangible, and existing only in contemplation of law." Dartmouth College v. Woodward, 4 Wheat (US) 518, 4 L.ed 629. The Supreme Court of Missouri has defined it as follows:

A corporation may be described as being an artificial being, existing only in contemplation of law; a legal entity, a fictitious person, vested by law with the capacity of taking and granting property and transacting business as an individual. It is composed of a number of individuals, authorized to act as if they were one person. The individual stockholders are the constituents or component parts through whose intelligence, judgment, and discretion the corporation acts. The affairs of a corporation cannot in many cases be conveniently conducted and managed by the stockholders, for they are often numerous and widely separated; yet they, in reality, compose the body corporate. [Jones v. Williams, et al., 139 Mo. 1, 39 S.W. 486, 490 (1897)]

Corporations fall into the following broad classifications: (1) public, (2) private, (3) quasi-public, (4) profit, (5) nonprofit, (6) foreign, and (7) domestic.

A *public corporation* is one created for public purposes only. It is connected with the administration of the government. Examples are states, school districts, cities, and counties. *Quasi-public* is a term applied to corporations which are not strictly public in the sense of being organized for governmental purposes. Quasi-public corporations are those that operate by contributing to the comfort, convenience, and welfare of the general public. Examples are gas, water, electric, and other utility companies. *Private corporations* are created for private purposes, as distinguished from purely public purposes, and are generally thought of as business entities carrying on activities for profit-making purposes. A *profit-making corporation* is primarily a business corporation organized with a view toward gains that are to be distributed among its members. A *nonprofit corporation,* sometimes referred to as eleemosynary, is one created for or devoted to charitable purposes of those supported by charity. *Foreign corporations* are those organized in another state or country, and a *domestic corporation* is one organized within the state. As we shall see later, it is not generally recommended that you organize your corporation in a foreign state or jurisdiction.

Basically, the character of a corporation is determined by the object of its formation and the nature of its business as stated in its articles of incorporation. The character of a corporation may not be changed by calling it something different from what is specified in its articles of incorporation. Because of this requirement, you should make certain that your articles of incorporation sufficiently describe and define the purposes for which the corporation is established.

**Advantages of Corporate Entity
Over Other Business Entities**

There are many factors you must consider when deciding which form of business organization you wish to use. Several factors have been discussed, but the following are the most significant reasons for adoption of the corporate form:

1. The owners, stockholders, or principals have no individual liability over than the capital contribution in stock payments.

2. Corporations are perpetual and can continue to exist until dissolved.

3. Corporations are a separate entity from the stockholders and can sue and be sued and hold and deal in property.

4. Stock can ordinarily be sold or otherwise transferred at will.

5. Corporations can raise capital by the issuance of new stock, bonds, or other securities.

6. A Board of Directors is the center of authority, acting by majority agreement.

7. As a separate entity, a corporation has credit possibilities apart from stockholders, and stock is sometimes available as collateral.

8. Corporations have flexibility in that the charter and bylaws can be easily changed.

9. The modern trend in the business world is toward greater use of the corporation to operate a business. This is a result of the natural and ever increasing exposure to personal liability, the ease with which one can form his corporation under the simplified state laws, and the many other advantages of incorporation.

10. The tax advantages of incorporation include the use of a corporation as a tax shelter, wealth building advantages under corporate pension and profit sharing plans, group life, medical, and hospital insurance coverage for owners, deductions for business losses, and others.

Where to Incorporate

Many years ago, it was considered advantageous to incorporate in some other state where there were more liberal laws for easy incorporation. This was called "corporate forum shopping." This practice is no longer advisable and has disadvantages rather than having any real advantages. Now it is almost universally accepted that the state of principal business activity is the state favored for incorporation.

The Partnership

The Uniform Partnership Act defines a partnership as "an association of two or more persons to carry on as co-owners a business for profit." This definition is now widely accepted in most of the states. Draftsmen of the act recognized that it is neither practical nor feasible to frame an exact and comprehensive definition of a partnership. This results, in part, from the fact that partnerships bear some resemblance to, and have certain features or characteristics in common with, various other groups, associations, transactions, or relationships. These distinctions are discussed later, and are important only for the purpose of giving you an understanding of the many situations in which you could become a partner without knowing it.

A more inclusive definition of partnerships, based upon their historical development, is that a partnership is a contract, express or implied, between two or more competent persons to place their money, effects, labor, or skill, or some or all of them, into business, and to divide the profits and bear the losses in certain proportions. As we shall see later, these definitions can be better understood and more easily applied when we recognize the essential criteria, tests, or indicia of partnerships. When the courts are presented with the question as to whether a partnership exists in specific fact situations, they generally look for four essentials.

1. Two or more parties intending to be partners;
2. Sharing of profits and losses;
3. Joint ownership and control of capital assets or property of the group; and
4. Joint control and management of the business.

The two main types of partnership are general and limited. *General partnerships* are further classified in some states as trading (or commercial) partnerships, and non-trading (or ordinary) partnerships. A limited partnership can be formed only by compliance with the statutory requirements.

A *trading partnership* is one engaged in the business of buying or selling for profit; any other partnership business is called a non-trading partnership. *Non-trading partnerships* include business or professional activities among attorneys, physicians, contractors, builders, farmers, plumbers, real estate brokers, insurance agents, and other service businesses or professions. Recent statutory enactments in some states authorize certain professional groups to form special professional corporations. These professional corporations are not partnerships, and you should not attempt to form these without professional advice.

A *dormant partner*, also known as a secret or silent partner, is generally one whose name is not used by the firm, and who is generally unknown to those dealing with the partnership. A *silent partner* is a person whose connection with the partnership business is concealed and does not generally take any active part in the business. Silent partners have the same general powers as ordinary partners and have the same right to act for the firm in partnership transactions in the absence of stipulations to the contrary. Therefore, such a partner may be liable for firm obligations as are other general partners.

The terms *junior partner* and *senior partner*, while frequently used in law firms and other professional partnerships, generally have no special legal significance other than such meaning as may be given to the terms in the

96

partnership agreement. In some states it is permissible for the partners, by written agreement, to establish various classes of nonpartner members, and others. The agreement may provide for their varying rights and duties in relation to the partnership. The rights, powers, and duties of junior partners, as distinguished from senior partners, may be set forth in the partnership agreement.

Limited Partnership

Most states have special statutes which authorize the formation of limited partnerships. These are special situations which permit individuals, upon complying with the statutory requirements, to contribute specific sums to the capital of a partnership firm, and then limit their liability to the amount of their capital contribution. This is somewhat like a corporation. A limited partnership is defined by the Uniform Limited Partnership Act to be a partnership formed by two or more persons under that act, having as members one or more general partners and one or more limited partners. The act specifically declares that limited partners, as such, are not bound by the obligations of the partnership. Each limited partnership consists of at least one general partner whose rights, powers, and obligations are similar to those of partners in an ordinary partnership, and at least one limited partner who is basically interested in investing, rather than participating in the business of the partnership.

The general purpose of the Uniform Limited Partnership Act, which has been adopted in all but three or four of the states, is to allow a form of business enterprise, other than a corporation, in which persons could invest their money without becoming liable as general partners for all debts of the partnership. A limited partner is in a position very similar to that of a shareholder of a corporation.

The Uniform Limited Partnership Act provides that a partnership may carry on any business which a partnership without limited partners may carry on, except those specified in the act. In most of these states a limited partnership may not engage in the banking or insurance business. In some states there are no limitations as to the kind of business in which a limited partnership may engage.

The general partner in a limited partnership has rights and powers similar to those possessed by the members of an ordinary general partnership, and may become individually liable for all the debts of the firm. He is accountable to other partners as a fiduciary. The act restricts the general partner's authority in a number of ways. It also provides that one may be a general partner and a limited partner in the same partnership at the same time. In this situation the partner has all the rights, powers, limitations, and liabilities of a general partner.

Although not specifically required by the Uniform Partnership Act, written Articles of Partnership are usually executed. These articles outline the contribution by the partners into the business, whether material or managerial, and generally delineate the roles of the partners in the business relationship. The following are example articles typically contained in a partnership agreement:

Name, Purpose, Domicile

Duration of Agreement

Performance by Partners

Character of Partners (general or limited, active or silent)

Contributions by Partners (at inception, at later date)

Business Expenses (how handled)

Authority (individual partner authority in conduct of business)

Separate Debts

Books, Records, and Method of Accounting

Division of Profits and Losses

Draws and Salaries

Rights of Continuing Partner

Death of a Partner (dissolution and winding up)

Employee Management

Release of Debts

Sale of Partnership Interests

Arbitration

Additions, Alterations, or Modifications of Partner-
ship Agreement
Settlement of Disputes
Required and Prohibited Acts
Absence and Disability

Business Trusts

A business trust is an unincorporated organization created for profit under a written instrument or declaration of trust, whose management is to be conducted by trustees for the benefit of persons whose legal interests are represented by transferable certificates of participation, or shares. The term business trust is sometimes referred to as a "Massachusetts Trust," or a "Common Law Trust."

The typical business trust has the following characteristics in common with a corporation:

1. *Associates.* Normally two or more persons are associated together in the enterprise; however, both a business trust and a corporation may have a sole shareholder.

2. *Objective.* The purpose of the business organization is to carry on a business and divide the profits from the business among the owners.

3. *Continuity of Life.* The death, bankruptcy, or withdrawal of a shareholder does not terminate the organization.

4. *Centralization of Management.* The trustee has continuing exclusive authority to make the management decisions necessary to the conduct of the business. The

shareholders of a business trust, like the shareholders of a corporation, may not ordinarily participate in the management.

5. *Free Transferability of Interests.* The interests of the shareholders are transferable without the consent of the other shareholders.

6. *Limited Liability.* Ordinarily, the beneficiaries of a trust are not personally liable to third persons on obligations incurred by the trustee in the administration of the trust. The trustee is personally liable, at least to the extent to which the trust estate is sufficient to indemnify him. While the trustee may look to the trust estate for reimbursement, he cannot pursue the beneficiaries unless there is an agreement by the beneficiaries to reimburse him. If there is such an agreement, third persons could, by a proceeding in equity, enforce their claims against the beneficiaries if the trustee fails to pay and the trust estate is insufficient. These principles of trust law are generally applicable to business trusts. It is a general rule that the beneficiaries are not personally liable if the trustee is a trustee and not an agent of the beneficiaries subject to their control and direction. The line between trust and agency is not always easy to draw. For this reason, draftsmen customarily include in the declaration of trust specific provisions as follows:

1. *Management.* The trustee shall have full power and discretion to manage the business and affairs of the trust.

2. *Limitations on Liability of Trustee and Beneficiaries.* Neither the trustee nor the beneficiaries shall be personally liable as partners or otherwise; but for debts the trustee shall be liable as trustee to the extent of the trust property only.

3. *Stipulations against Personal Liability.* The trustee shall insert in every contract a stipulation that neither he nor the beneficiaries shall be personally liable, but that all persons dealing with the trustee shall look only to the property of the trust for payment.

4. *Control.* The cases are not uniform as to the effect of various provisions that might be interpreted to give the beneficiaries ultimate control over the trustee. Liberal authority has permitted beneficiaries to terminate the trust, to amend or alter the trust agreement, to elect trustees annually and fill vacancies, and to remove trustees and elect new ones, without subjecting the beneficiaries to unlimited liability. Other cases have reached a different result. As a matter of prudence these powers, in respect to the administration of the trust, should not be reserved to the beneficiaries unless the governing law is clearly in accord with the liberal view.

The business trust was originally used in Massachusetts for the purpose of dealing in and developing real estate. The corporate form of organization could not be used because Massachusetts statutes did not permit a corporation to be organized for that purpose. Soon the use of the business trust was extended to other states and to other fields of activity. For purposes of convenience they are classified as land trusts, trusts for ownership of property, trusts for carrying on business, investment trusts, and liquidation trusts.

The statutes of some states expressly recognize the existence of business trusts, and in some instances regulate them as they do corporations. In other states the statutes define the term corporation to include all associations having any powers or privileges not possessed by individuals or partnerships, thus including business trusts. The effect of these statutes is to deprive the business trust of most, if not all, of its exemptions from the burdens placed upon the corporate form of doing business. As a consequence, the motivation for organizing business trusts in some states has diminished.

The Business Trust and Income Taxes

The Internal Revenue Code prescribes certain classes into which various organizations fall for purposes of income taxation. These classes are: corporations, partnerships, and trusts. The term *corporation* is broadly defined in the code as any "associations, joint-stock companies, and insurance companies."

The term *association* refers to an organization whose characteristics require it to be classified as a corporation rather than as another type of organization such as a

103

partnership or a trust. The I.R.S. lists six major characteristics which distinguish a corporation from other organizations. These are (1) associates, (2) an objective to carry on business and divide the gains therefrom, (3) continuity of life, (4) centralization of management, (5) liability for corporate debts limited to corporate property, and (6) free transferability of interest.

Whether a particular organization is to be classified as an association and taxed as a corporation must be determined by taking into account the presence or absence of each of these corporate characteristics. Of these characteristics the last four, continuity of life, centralization of management, liability for corporate debts, and free transferability of interest, are generally common to trusts. Accordingly, whether a trust is to be treated for tax purposes as a trust or as a corporation depends upon whether there are associates, and an objective to carry on business and divide the gains.

Joint Venture

A joint venture is an association of two or more persons to carry out a single business enterprise for profit, for which purpose they combine their property, money, efforts, skill, and knowledge. It is a special combination of two or more persons, where, in some specific adventure, a profit is jointly sought, without any actual partnership or corporate designation. It is ordinarily, but not necessarily, limited to a single transaction, which serves to distinguish it from a partnership. However, the business of conducting it to a successful termination may continue for an extended period of time. A joint venture, while not identical with a partnership, is so similar in its nature and in the relations created that the rights of the parties as between themselves are governed, in most instances, by the same rules that govern partnerships.

The establishment of a joint venture requires the elements of contribution by the parties, a single undertaking, joint property and management interests, and the right of all parties to profits. A contract is essential to the creation of a joint venture, although it may be an oral contract, as the legal concept is not created by law, but it is voluntarily assumed.

The rights, duties, and obligations of the parties to a joint venture agreement are determined by the language of the agreement, although there are some general principles that apply. These include a necessity for accounting between the parties, a winding up of affairs on dissolution of the joint venture, and an equal division of any profits, in the absence of any contrary provisions in the agreement.

Agency

Agency is the fiduciary relationship resulting from the manifestation of consent by one person, the principal, to another, the agent, that the agent shall manage some business to be transacted in the principal's name or on his account and subject to the control of the principal, and consent by the agent to do such business and render an account of it. The term agency implies commercial or contractual dealings between two parties by and through the medium of another. It is a fiduciary relationship by which one person, the principal, confides to another, the agent, the management of some business to be transacted in the principal's name or on his account. The agent acts for, and derives his authority from, the principal.

Agency is ordinarily a contractual relationship created by agreement based upon a consideration. However, it may be gratuitous, or it may be created by estoppel insofar as third persons are concerned. That is, it may arise from acts and appearances that lead third persons to believe that an agency relationship exists. When a third person has relied on such appearances to his detriment, the principal or agent is estopped from denying the agency.

A principal whose agent has violated or threatened to violate his duties may, under most circumstances, cancel the agency contract or refuse to pay the agreed compensation. An exception may exist when the agency contract is coupled with an interest running to the agent. The principal's remedy may also be an action for money in the hands of the agent had and received on behalf of the principal, an action on the contract for a breach or failure to perform it, or an action to recover damages for tortious conduct of the agent. If the action is for money, a default and a prior demand and refusal may have to occur before bringing an action. Where the breach of the agency contract also constitutes a tort, the principal may elect either remedy, or in some states, both. Equitable remedies, including an action for an accounting, are also available because of the fiduciary relationship.

The limit of liability of an agent to his principal for breach of the agency agreement is the loss or damage which naturally results from the agent's acts.

A principal is legally responsible for the acts of the agent performed within the scope of the authority granted. The agency relationship can generally be created orally or in writing; or it may be implied from the acts of the parties. A power of attorney or other agency to convey real estate generally has to be in writing, as well as any other activities within the statute of frauds. It is always a good idea to have most agreements in writing. A general power of attorney, in the absence of statutes, requires that a power of attorney to convey real property or any interest in it must be acknowledged with the same formalities as a deed or mortgage.

An agent is different from an employee in that he has authority to bind his principal in a general sense, while an employee generally is employed to accomplish certain specified duties. An agent and an employee are also different from an independent contractor in that the principal or employer has control over agents and employees and can direct them in their duties, while the principal does not have control over the activities of an independent contractor in the performance of the work required under a contract. The fact that a principal reserves the right to inspect the work, or that the principal's architect has the right to require the redoing of work that does not meet contract specifications, does not give such control over the independent contractor as to make him merely an employee. In other words, the reserved power and right to determine and ensure compliance with the terms of the contract does not constitute control of how the work is to be done.

Although a real estate broker is sometimes called a real estate "agent," a broker is not an agent because he does not have authority to make a contract with a third person that will bind his client. A *bailee* is a person to whom property is delivered or transferred under an agreement whereby the property is to be returned to the owner or to others. Thus, a bailee is not an agent as he does not have authority to make a contract with a third person that will bind the owner.

An agency can be created to perform any act which the principal could lawfully do. The subject matter of an agency contract may not be illegal or against public policy. Thus, a court will not enforce an agency contract by which one person is employed to do an illegal act.

There are some acts which cannot be done by, or through an agent, for example, voting, testifying in court, making a will, acknowledging documents, and so on.

There are several kinds of agents. A general agent is authorized to transact all of his principal's affairs in connection with a particular kind of business or trade, or to transact all of his business at a certain place. A special agent is authorized by the principal to handle a definite business transaction or to do a specific act. A universal agent is authorized by the principal to do all acts that can be delegated lawfully to representatives. This form of agency arises, for example, where a person gives another person a blanket power of attorney to do anything that may be done within the scope of the agency.

Attorney at Law

In the most general sense the term *attorney* means an agent or substitute, or one who is appointed and authorized to act in the place of another. The term *attorney-in-fact* is frequently used to describe this relationship.

Attorney at law (the lawyer) is an advocate, counsel, or official agent employed in preparing, managing, and trying cases in the courts.

The right of an attorney to practice law is governed in each state by state statutes and court rules. The right of an attorney to practice law, once he gets his license, may be revoked if he engages in conduct that makes him unfit to hold a license or to exercise the duties and responsibilities of an attorney.

Contracts employing attorneys are generally of two types:

1. *Contingent fee contracts.* This is a contract under which the amount of fee payable to the attorney is contingent on the amount to be recovered, either by settlement or judgment.

2. *Contract amount.* This is an arrangement by which fees are payable regardless of whether or not there is any recovery. This is also sometimes called a "fixed fee" contract. Also some contracts are based solely on an hourly rate.

One of the most important aspects of a fee agreement with a lawyer, as in other contracts, is to have it in writing and make certain you fully understand what the lawyer is to do for you and that he fully understands what you want him to do for you. A lack of communication between lawyers and clients about fee arrangements contributes a great deal to the adverse attitude many people have about lawyers.

Distributors

Salesmen, factors, distributors and dealers are engaged in a common pursuit, the distribution of goods. They have each on occasion been described as agents and their contracts as involving employment.

A *salesmen* sells property on behalf of his principal, title passing directly from the owner or manufacturer to the customer, the buyer. Similarly, a *factor* acts as agent for another, but he differs from a salesman in that he generally has possession of the goods delivered under a consignment agreement. A *distributor* is also in effect a sales representative, but he sells on behalf of himself, having purchased the goods from the manufacturer. Likewise, a *dealer* sells on his own behalf. However, a distributor ordinarily sells at wholesale to dealers, while the dealer ordinarily sells at retail.

Good Will

Good will is the benefit or advantage accruing to an establishment beyond the mere physical asset value, and arising out of public patronage and encouragement. It is an intangible which cannot be separated from the business operation. Its basic components are continuity of place, reputation and name. Its essence lies in the capacity of a business to attract trade, and therefore it applies to competitive businesses. Good will can be bought and sold in connection with a going business.

A dictionary definition of good will is that it is the favor which the management of a business wins from the public; the fixed and favorable consideration of customers arising from an established and well conducted business.

Assignment for the Benefit of Creditors

Generally, an assignment for the benefit of creditors is bad news! Bad news for everybody—debtor, creditors, lawyers, accountants, bystanders. This involves a transfer by a debtor of substantially all of his property to an assignee, without consideration from the assignee, who holds it in trust and collects the amount owing to the debtor, sells and conveys the property, distributes the proceeds of all the property among the debtor's creditors, and returns the surplus, if any, to the debtor. Rarely is there a surplus; seldom are all creditors paid.

Such assignments are generally provided for by state statutes (but are not frequently used), and are subject, in some respects, to the federal Bankruptcy Act.

You should carefully review your own state statutes and get legal advice about potential application of the Bankruptcy Acts.

6

Estate Planning

What Is Estate Planning?

The term or phrase estate planning has undergone an expanding series of definitions during the past few years. It means different things to different people. To the professional estate planner or to a lawyer who specializes in estate planning, it means estate tax savings, reduction of transfer costs, and other items associated with wealthy people. To you and me it may simply mean the avoidance of all probate proceedings. To a person 21 years of age it has a different meaning and significance than it does to a person 91 years of age; and there is a big difference for rich people and for poor people.

From whatever view you have of your estate, and your need for estate planning, this discussion is designed not for the professional estate planner, but for you and your family and friends to examine the need for estate planning and how to do it.

Estate planning, for our purposes, consists of a conscious, positive, and active undertaking by you to evaluate and analyze your estate, your taking steps to earn more, save more, and retain more in your estate, your plans to effectively use, spend and invest your assets, and making specific but flexible plans for transferring those assets during and after your lifetime. It is simply a plan for building your estate, accumulating more capital, increasing the value of your assets, keeping it, using it, giving it away, and making it available to your dependents, friends, charitable institutions, and the government, and making an intelligent, economical transfer after you are finished with it. For those who do not have a taxable estate, the avoidance of probate and its unnecessary costs, delays, and frustration may be one of the most important objectives.

Is Estate Planning Necessary?

Your estate planning should include the preparation in writing of all available information about you, your assets, income, and income-producing abilities and potential, an analysis of all current assets, the potential for future accumulation of assets, and an intelligent, pre-planned program for conserving, increasing and using it during your life. It should be reviewed periodically, at least once each year, and after any significant changes in your family or financial situation, and you should have specific alternative plans in the event death should intervene at any stage. Plan for yourself, your family and others.

During your planning process you should consider the following:

1. How your income and assets may be shifted to reduce future liabilities;

2. Accumulate sufficient liquid assets to cover all future liabilities;

3. Make plans for accumulation of sufficient capital so that investment income will adequately meet family needs in all circumstances;

4. Prepare a plan by which capital may be used in an orderly manner in the event it should be necessary in the future to supplement income; and

5. Crystallize your thinking, discuss your plans with adult members of your family, your trustees, your named executor, and any business partners or associates so that there should never be a crash and burn situation; and

6. Where appropriate arrange the ownership of your estate so that probate proceedings will not delay and reduce the distribution to your successors.

You should not get emotional about estate planning or think estate planning means death. In fact, if you have a good plan your longevity may well be enhanced. And you do not necessarily have to pay a big estate planning fee or lawyers' fees to develop a good estate plan.

Most estate planning discussions, of necessity, revolve around the payment of taxes and probate costs. You owe it to yourself and to your family to plan in such a way that money doesn't needlessly go to the government in unnecessary taxes, or to lawyers and estate planners in situations where it can be avoided.

Estate Tax Planning

The Tax Reform Act of 1976 has completely revolutionized estate planning for most Americans. Estate planning has always revolved around the significant, important, and ever-present tax problems presented to the professional estate planners, or tax experts. The new code raised the exemptions on estate and gift taxes so that most Americans are now totally exempted from them. In fact, reliable estimates are that over 97 percent of American citizens will be exempted from estate taxes because of the higher exemptions. Even if your estate exceeds the exemption amounts, you can avoid all estate taxes through proper estate planning.

Before 1976 the basic estate tax exemption was $60,000; the marital deduction was 50 percent of the value of the adjusted gross estate. The gift tax exemption was $30,000 plus the annual $3,000 per donee exclusion. The Tax Reform Act of 1976 introduced a single unified estate and gift tax rate schedule with progressive rates based on cumulative transfers during lifetime and at death. The amount of the estate tax is determined under the new law by applying the unified rates to the cumulative lifetime and deathtime transfers and then subtracting the taxes payable on the lifetime transfers. Since the estate tax bracket depends on cumulative lifetime and deathtime transfers, the result is that taxpayers who transfer their property during life and those who keep their property until death are treated substantially the same way for transfer tax purposes. Thus, the gift during life may not now reduce the gift taxes, but the exemptions are higher and you can still save on estate taxes if you plan properly.

Under the old code, gifts made within three years of death were included in the gross estate unless the estate could prove they were not made in contemplation of death. Under the new code, all transfers made within three years of death are includable in the gross estate, regardless of the decedent's motives. Thus, you can still save on estate taxes by making gifts, but you must do it in a different way.

The unified credit schedule was phased in over a five-year period, and after 1980 the exemption will be $175,625 per person for unmarried people. The marital deduction was significantly changed.

Marital Deduction

The new martial deduction is the greater of $250,000 or 50 percent of the adjusted gross estate. The $250,000 deduction may be taken irrespective of the 50 percent limitation. The adjusted gross estate is the gross estate less debts, expenses and losses.

117

The deduction, of course, is limited to the value of any amount which is passing or has passed from the decedent to the surviving spouse. The marital deduction applies to gifts to a spouse during lifetime as well as dispositions at death. Of course, a married person is also entitled to the individual exemption of $175,625 in addition to the marital deduction.

The new marital deduction provision is

(A)   In general—the aggregate amount of the deductions allowed under this section (computed without regard to this subsection) shall not exceed the greater of—
(i) $250,000; or
(ii)   50 percent of the value of the adjusted gross estate (as defined in paragraph (2)).

By way of example, suppose a decedent left an adjusted gross estate of $300,000. Under the old code the marital deduction would have been limited to $150,000 (50 percent of $300,000). But under the new code $250,000 can be taken plus the $175,625.

The new code also provides for an unlimited gift tax marital deduction for the first $100,000 in lifetime gifts to a spouse. Gifts after $100,000 up to $200,000 to a spouse are fully taxed and a 50 percent marital deduction is allowed for gifts over $200,000. Under these new tax measures it is easy to transfer up to $525,625 without any estate or gift taxes being imposed. For example, a person with an estate of $525,625 could make a lifetime gift of $100,000 to the spouse (fully exempt) and leave the balance of

$425,625 (or at least $250,000) to the surviving spouse. The $100,000 gift during lifetime is exempt. The $250,000 exemption would apply to the property left to the surviving spouse leaving the balance of $175,625—the amount of the basic exemption. In this example, however, planning should concern not only the estate of the first spouse to die, but the surviving spouse who would have some new estate tax problems to solve.

Congress fully recognized the inequity and hardship caused by the old laws, especially as applied to farmers and family-owned businesses. The new tax code gives substantial benefits and reductions in estate taxes to farms and other closely held businesses. The new tax code allows an executor to elect to value real property used for farming or in a closely held business, based on its current value as a farm or as a closely held business, rather than on the basis of its potential "highest and best" use for other purposes, as under the old code. The "special use" valuation cannot reduce the gross estate by more than $500,000. Methods for valuing qualified property are provided, and there are various rules and limitations on the application of this section of the code.

Because of the higher exemptions for gift and estate taxes under the new code, many more people will be able to plan estates and write wills without any significant tax problems. It is to your advantage to know about these new laws and to know how to take advantage of them.

Some states impose estate taxes, and you should take these into account although they are less important than the federal code. They vary from state to state and you will want to look at them as part of your estate planning.

Steps In Estate Planning

Here are the most important steps you should consider in your estate planning:

1. *Inventory.* Prepare a complete inventory of your assets, your current income and any increments in assets or income which you can reasonably expect in the future, whether by inheritance gifts, or otherwise. List all your assets giving the base cost, date of acquisition, the current values and estimated values at various future intervals. List all your life insurance, group policies, and other coverage, giving the cash values and face values. The valuation of business interests can be difficult, but you should be realistic in evaluating the potential future income. Your list of assets should include those of all members of your family, and indicate the form of ownership. A separate list can be made for other family members, and it should include the sources of the property with value estimates. Your plan may not be adequate if you do not have all the assets and potential assets included. This inventory will not only help you plan for the future, it will give you a good picture of where you are now. You can reach your goals and objectives much easier

if you have a clear picture of where you have been, where you are now, and where you wish to go. Writing it down on paper also helps you crystallize your thinking about how you can reach your goals and objectives.

2. *Classify Your Assets.* Classification of your assets usually falls into three general categories: (1) cash; (2) assets that can be converted into cash; and (3) assets that will remain as capital. The amount of cash that can be raised with each asset and the problem of converting assets into cash should be analyzed and discussed with adult members of your family. The tax costs which may result on liquidation of assets must be considered. Your analysis of your assets and how they may be utilized in various contingencies is a very significant family transaction and you should help the other members of your family discuss it objectively and intelligently without being emotionally distraught.

3. *Debts and Claims.* An estimate of the amount of debts and claims that will evolve in the estate should be made. This estimate should include current income tax liabilities, debts, funeral and last illness expenses, and administration costs. As you review these items of cost you should consider all methods to eliminate most of the unnecessary probate costs.

4. *Estate Liabilities.* After deducting from the estimated total value of the assets at death the estimated debts and claims, you can determine the estate tax liability that

will probably be due, if any. One of the principal reasons for having good estate plans is to avoid estate taxes. After the enactment of the Tax Reform Act of 1976 with the higher exemptions, most of us will be exempt; but you need to plan in advance. If your taxable estate exceeds the exemptions, you should plan accordingly. Potential claims against your estate should be evaluated from time to time, and appropriate plans should be made to adequately handle all such claims and debts.

5. *Liquidation of Estate Liabilities.* Make a schedule for the liquidation of estate liabilities. This exercise should include your spouse and executor. Apply cash amounts from the list of cash assets and assets convertible into cash against the schedules of debts, claims, administration costs and estate tax liabilities, if any, and compute the income tax cost on the liquidation of the assets. Then see whether there is enough cash left to meet the cash needs of the family during the administration of the estate. This comparison of cash available to the estate will indicate whether it may be necessary for a conversion of other assets to handle the estate costs. These steps may seem hypothetical to you, but you need to know the facts before you can determine what problems need solving.

6. *Avoiding Probate.* If you have a taxable estate you should consider the assignment of the remaining assets, or a part of them, to individuals or trusts. You should make your choice as to whether the potential tax liabili-

ties are sufficient to motivate you to make an appropriate transfer or use some other method to avoid taxes. For those who have a potentially large taxable estate, professional advice should be obtained.

7. *Beneficiaries.* Prepare a schedule showing the assets that will be in the hands of each beneficiary after distribution; this list should also include the separately owned property of each beneficiary. The annual income available from these sources should be compared with the amount of annual income which you have determined should be available for each beneficiary. The inheritance taxes of your state, if any, should be considered in evaluating the interests of each beneficiary.

8. *Reduction of Liabilities.* Consider other methods of reducing liabilities. For example, lifetime gifts can still reduce estate tax liability by removing future appreciation in value from your estate, and increase assets and income available to members of your family. You may wish to get professional advice where significant tax problems are involved.

9. *Transfer of Assets.* Consider the transfer of income-producing properties to other members of your family, or to a family corporation or partnership to save income taxes as well as estate taxes. Consider also the use of a private annuity, Clifford Trust, or other methods of tax saving.

10. *Retirement.* Make long range plans for your own retirement.

Conserving and Managing Your Estates

The term estate planning almost always suggests death and taxes. Although taxes, in a taxable estate, are important, and the disposition of property after death is a major factor in estate planning, there is much more involved in the acquisition, planning, holding, using, maintaining, and managing of your estate.

Planning an estate may consist entirely, in the beginning, of getting an estate. How well you assemble your estate, and how well you maintain it, use it, and conserve it may answer most of the main questions and the "death and taxes" problems that come later. Or the taxes can be avoided altogether if you make the right moves at the right time. The primary emphasis in this chapter is on the proper evaluation of a non-taxable estate, and the disposition of property where there are no significant tax problems. However, we will discuss briefly some of the other factors and information you may wish to consider in assembling, managing, holding, using, and transferring your property.

Joint Ownership of Property

Typically, married couples have the title to their home and other real estate in joint ownership. There are several types of concurrent ownership methods.

Tenancies by the Entirety

This exists only where the co-owners are husband and wife. Upon the death of either spouse, the survivor-

124

ship cannot be destroyed during the lives of the co-owners except with the consent of both. In some states, this form of ownership exists only with respect to real property; in a few states it may exist in the case of personal property.

Joint Tenancies

Joint tenancies are not limited to husband and wife; however, the two forms of ownership are similar in that the right of survivorship exists in each. In a joint tenancy one of the co-owners may transfer his or her undivided interest in the property during his or her lifetime.

Tenancies in Common

In a tenancy in common, which is not limited to husband and wife, there is no right of survivorship. Either co-owner may dispose of his or her undivided interest in the property during his or her life, or by will.

Community Property

Community property laws vary in the different states where community property exists. It is advisable to check the law of the particular state regarding questions which may arise. The community property states are Arizona, California, Idaho, Louisiana, Nevada, New Mexico, Texas, and Washington.

Although writers and legal scholars argue the pros and cons of joint ownership of property, common sense tells us that there are no major objections, in the average estate to these forms of ownership; it is the most commonly used by married persons. This is especially true in the non-taxable estate. Unless some unusual objection arises, joint ownership is generally the best method for married couples to employ. The major part of a married person's estate generally goes to the surviving spouse, whether by will or by operation of law; therefore, the "probate" of a family home, in most instances, is absurd.

Insurance

The proceeds of life insurance are ordinarily includable in the gross estate of the insured for estate tax purposes when the proceeds are receivable by the estate of the insured or when the insured possessed at his death any of the incidents of ownership in the policy. Where the insurance proceeds are large and may have the effect of increasing the estate to a taxable amount, it may be appropriate to consider ways of eliminating the proceeds from the gross estate. The usual methods for accomplishing this are: (1) assign the policies irrevocably to other persons, such as members of your family; (2) assign the policies irrevocably to a trust; (3) arrange for ownership of the policies as part of a qualified employee benefit plan; or (5) elect during life to receive the cash value of the policies and use it up. Typically, a married person designates the spouse as primary beneficiary of a life insurance policy, and having the spouse own the policy is quite simple.

126

Two of the most overlooked items in estate planning programs are (1) the failure to review the plans periodically, and (2) the failure to discuss the plans with family members and business associates so that they may be advised of your plans and intentions.

7

Avoiding Probate

The living trust has become very popular during the past few years as a device in estate planning and in "probate avoidance." The utilization of the living trust as a tool for avoiding excessive legal fees and probate costs has captured the imagination of a major portion of the general public in this country. The joint ownership of property and other probate avoidance techniques were discussed in Chapter 6.

Until recently it was generally thought that a trust agreement was functional only for the wealthy, those who created trusts primarily to avoid probate costs and taxes. For a wide variety of reasons, the trust arrangement, especially the revocable trust, has caught on like wildfire with American citizens. Now, almost everybody is jumping on the bandwagon to avoid what many consider to be the "probate rip-off." Many people just find it utterly incredible that they can convey property from one person to another during their lifetime at practically no transfer cost, while it takes years and years in the probate system to make the same transfer, and the costs, fees, delays, and court proceedings are staggering!

Without fanning the flames of controversy about the use of trust in probate avoidance, and without giving my subjective, or objective, views of the traditional probate system, let us (1) look at the advantages of the use of the revocable trust, and (2) discuss how you can use the living trust to assist you in your overall estate planning.

The Revocable Living Trust

A trust is a legal relationship in which one person conveys property to a second person for the benefit of a third person. The person creating the trust is called the *Grantor, Trustor* or *Settlor;* the person or entity having legal title to the trust property is the *Trustee;* and the person for whose benefit it is created, the one having the equitable interest in the trust property, is called the *Beneficiary.* You can be Grantor, Trustee and Beneficiary all at the same time in some situations.

There are many kinds or classes of trusts in addition to the living trust; for example, trusts are called testamentary, constructive, resulting, charitable, active, passive, contingent, dry, educational, executory, implied, involuntary, naked, simple, complex, shifting, secret, Totten, and many other names. However, we are here concerned with the living trust and its use in your estate planning to avoid unnecessary probate costs.

A revocable living trust is an arrangement wherein an individual places property, frequently income producing, in trust, naming himself or some other person or entity (for example, a bank or trust company) as trustee or co-trustee, but reserving the right to revoke the trust so that the trust property can be returned to him on such revocation. An irrevocable trust is one which is not revocable by the Grantor; it is final; it cannot be altered.

Advantages of a Revocable Living Trust

In the typical revocable living trust, a Grantor transfers property to a Trustee under a written agreement. This agreement provides for the Trustee to pay the Grantor all of the income from the trust during his lifetime, altogether with such amounts of principal as may be requested by the Grantor. It also provides that the Grantor can amend or revoke the trust or change the Trustee at any time.

Upon the death of the Grantor, the trust becomes irrevocable, meaning that the terms of the trust cannot thereafter be changed. The trust property is held, administered, and distributed as if it has passed under the Grantor's will through probate and into a testamentary trust—all without the costs and delays of probate. The provisions of the trust agreement which apply to the administration and distribution of the trust assets after the death of the Grantor become operative and are carried out immediately. There are no probate delays, no probate costs, no fees or probate proceedings, and there is no publicity or spreading of facts upon the public probate records.

The revocable living trust is the answer to most of these problems. The Trustee can perform all of the necessary management of the trust assets, including the collection of income, the purchase and sale of trust assets, and the management of a closely held business or real estate. In an emergency, the Trustee can make payment of hospital, nursing and doctor bills, and any other expenses of the Grantor. The trust can be revoked by the Grantor if he so desires, or the Grantor may actively manage the trust property while leaving the legal title in the name of the Trustee. If the Grantor dies, the trust can act as a substitute for the Grantor's will insofar as the assets of the trust are concerned.

There are a wide variety of advantages to the revocable living trust in estate planning, including the following:

1. Reduction or elimination of unnecessary and excessive probate expenses, fees, costs and proceedings;
2. Privacy of disposition of assets at death;
3. Avoidance of a will contest;
4. Professional management capabilities;
5. Avoidance of probate in other states;
6. Uninterrupted management at death;
7. Segregation of assets;
8. Trial run for the trustee; and
9. Management uninterrupted by incapacity.

Tax Treatment of Revocable Living Trusts

Assets in a revocable living trust are taxable under the federal income, estate, and gift tax laws—and also under many state inheritance tax laws—in the same manner as property owned outright by the Grantor. No gift tax is payable when a Grantor creates a revocable living trust. During his lifetime all the income of the trust is taxed to him, and upon his death all of the property in the trust is included in his estate for federal estate and state inheritance tax purposes. After the Grantor's death the trust becomes irrevocable, and the same tax advantages available to a testamentary trust are available to the living trust. These include the avoidance of a second federal estate and state inheritance tax on the spouse's estate and the advantage of providing several different entities for income tax purposes.

Community Property and Revocable Living Trusts

If community property is to be placed in a revocable trust, the wife should join the husband in the execution of the trust agreement. In community property states, you should check the specific laws of your state on this question.

Irrevocable Living Trusts

Since the irrevocable trust is an outright gift, it provides further savings in estate taxes, if properly prepared, subject to the three year transfer before death rule. In other words, gifts made within three years of death are taxable in the estate; those before three years are not taxed.

Short Term Irrevocable Trusts: Clifford Trusts

An excellent method for saving on income taxes, but not estate or gift taxes, is the use of the short term irrevocable trust. Here the Grantor transfers income-producing property to a Trustee for a period in excess of ten years, retaining to himself the reversionary interest after the term of the trust. During the trust term, the income of the trust is paid to the beneficiary or accumulated in the trust and taxed to the beneficiaries or to the trust, usually at lower rates. These trusts are often used to accumulate income for minor children, which is subsequently utilized for their college education or other purposes, or for elderly persons who generally have a lower tax bracket.

Another excellent probate avoidance technique is the Private Annuity, discussed in *How To Use or Avoid Probate*, another of the publications of the Citizens Law Library. Sample forms for trusts are also provided in that volume.

8

The Layman's Guide to Writing a Will

There is a great myth in our society that one must have a lawyer to prepare a will. When I was in active law practice, I did nothing to dispel this erroneous notion; nor did any of my colleagues, as far as I could tell. Nonetheless, it is a myth.

You do not always need a lawyer; you can prepare your own will and plan your own estate unless you have (1) some unusual or extraordinary legal problem or (2) significant tax problems. The basis for the myth is, in part, that you don't always know how to determine whether you have one of these problems, and most people cling to the idea that they must have a lawyer do it for them. At any rate, if you do not have one of these problems, you can write your own will. A vast majority of the adult population in this nation can write their own wills by following these instructions. Statistics show that about 87½ percent of the adult population in this country do not have a will! Are you one of them?

First, however, let me explain what is meant by unusual or extraordinary legal problems and serious tax problems for those few who should not do it themselves. An unusual or extraordinary problem which generally requires attention from a specialist includes such situations as the following.

Antenuptial Agreements

It is most unusual for a person about to be married not to want his spouse to have a part of his estate. However, this does happen and where there is such an agreement, usually for tax consideration, you will generally need some assistance from a lawyer. During the past few years the concept of cohabitation or "living together" has become fairly common. In those states where common law marriages are valid, the antenuptial agreement may be considered as an overall part of estate planning. You may need legal advice on some aspects of antenuptial agreements to assure that they are valid.

Incompetent Dependents

Where one has incompetent dependents, special arrangements and attention by way of trusts, management, and other services are frequently required.

Bitter, Hostile, Divorce Proceedings

No one can help much here, but these kinds of cases require a lawyer to handle the sticky situations more than the writing of a will after the problems are resolved, if ever.

Expectation of Future Inheritance or Wealth

We all hope for these situations, and when it happens to you it would be advisable to obtain the services of a lawyer to assist in the preparation of your will.

Second Marriages

Two or more marriages, with free-floating anxiety and hostility involving former spouses and children from one or more prior marriages, can cause more problems than a host of lawyers can solve, but you had better get all the help you can in these cases.

In terms of writing wills and estate planning, serious tax problems generally denote an estate large enough to be taxable under the applicable estate tax codes. Under the new tax laws the exemptions are now much higher, and if you are single and have an estate in excess of $175,625, or are married with over $525,625, you may have serious tax consequences in your estate planning and will writing, in which case you should retain a professional.

As we have indicated, less than 3 percent of the population in this nation have assets sufficient to generate a taxable estate (for federal estate tax purposes) under the new code. Under these circumstances almost everyone except the 3 percent, and those with unusual problems, can write their own wills.

Before we get to the procedures for writing wills, let me make one more observation about lawyers. One of the most embarrassing and well-founded complaints against attorneys is that the turgid language they use in legal documents leads to perplexity, obscurity, and confusion. This is especially true in the case of wills, because attorneys seem obsessed with using the language they learned in law school as though there were some magic to the high sounding phrases. I must confess that I did this for many years.

For example, I remember the clause in the will form books, "I give, devise and bequeath all the rest, residue, and remainder of my estate, real, personal, or mixed, whatsoever and wheresoever located, to my beloved wife, Emily Jane Howell, formerly Emily Jane Gifford." Most form books use it, most attorneys I have known use it, most writers and professors use it, and I have used it. Nonetheless, I think it is better merely to say: "I give the residue of my estate to my wife Jane."

In the forms, clauses, and phrases used in this chapter, I will try to speak in plain English instead of the "lawyer language," and you should feel free to improve upon the simplicity of the language used if you deem it proper. The ultimate objective is for you to write a will which accurately expresses your desires and intentions in the disposition of your property.

Here are the procedures for writing your own will. The usual provisions of a will include some, but not all, of the following: (1) introductory clause to identify the testator; (2) special instructions, if any; (3) appointment of fiduciaries; (4) specific gifts; (5) general gifts; (6) residuary clause; (7) trust for minor children; (8) tax apportionment clause; (9) marital deduction clause, if applicable; (10) common disaster clause, usually for married couples with minor children; (11) execution (signing); and (12) attestation and signatures of witnesses.

Each of these parts, with suggested language, will be listed and discussed briefly. Alternative or additional clauses are also listed in the event you need them.

Introductory Clause

Immediately preceding the Introductory Clause is the title of the document which is usually as follows:

LAST WILL AND TESTAMENT
OF
JOHN DOE
I, John Doe, of Boulder, Colorado, make this my will and revoke my prior wills and codicils.

The esssential function of this part of the will is to identify the testator and to express an intention to make a will, and to revoke prior wills.

Special Instructions

I direct that my body shall be cremated after my death.

This part is not necessary, and it is frequently recommended that it be omitted entirely. It is not necessary to direct the payment of debts because the law requires it. It is my recommendation that you not use it, but that these instructions be made separate and apart from your will. A separate writing is sufficient.

Appointment of Fiduciaries
(Executor/Executrix, Trustee/Guardian)

Executor/Executrix

I appoint my wife, Jane Doe, Executrix of this, my Last Will. If my wife shall fail to qualify, or having qualified, shall die, resign, or cease to act as Executrix, then I appoint my son, Tom Doe, as executor in her place and stead. In case of the death, incapacity, or refusal to act of both, I appoint The First National Bank and Trust Company of _____ , as Executor.

Trustee

I appoint my brother, Tim Doe, Trustee under this my will. If my brother shall fail to qualify, or having qualified, shall die, resign or cease to act for any reason, I appoint my sister, Kim Doe, in place of my brother. If my sister shall fail to qualify, or having qualified, shall die, resign, or cease to act for any reason, I appoint the First National Bank and Trust Company of _____ as Trustee.

Guardian

If my spouse should not survive me, I name Polly Payton of the City of Boulder, Colorado, Guardian of the person of any of my children during their minority. If she fails to act or ceases to act as Guardian, I name Willy Manning of Boulder, Colorado, as Guardian, of the person of any of my children who are minors at the time.

Specific Gifts

I give my five karat, round, solitaire diamond ring with two baguettes to my daughter, Linda Doe, if she shall survive me.

I give my law books, office equipment, and all property contained in my law office to my son, Tom Doe, if he shall survive me.

General Gifts

I give the sum of Five Thousand Dollars ($5,000) to my brother, Tim Doe, if he shall survive me.

Residuary Clause

I give the residue of my estate to my wife, Jane, if she survives me. If my wife, Jane, predeceases me, I give said property, in equal shares, to my three children, Tom, Linda, and Ann, share and share alike, per stirpes.

Common Disaster Clause

If any beneficiary and I should die in a common accident or disaster or under such circumstances that it is doubtful who died first [or within 30, 60, 90, days of my death], then all the provisions of this will shall take effect as if such beneficiary had in fact predeceased me.

Execution

In Witness Whereof, I have hereunto set my hand and seal this ____ day of December, 19__ .

(Signature)

Attestation and Signature of Witnesses

The foregoing instrument, consisting of two (2) type-written pages, including this page, was signed, sealed, published and declared by the said John Doe as his Last Will and Testament, in the presence of each of us, who at his request and in his presence and in the presence of one another, subscribe our names hereto as witnesses on the day of the date hereof; and we declare that at the time of the execution of this instrument the said John Doe according to our best knowledge and belief, was of sound and disposing mind and memory and under no constraint.

_____ residing at _____
_____

_____ residing at _____
_____

_____ residing at _____
_____

Additional or Alternative Clauses

There may be some additional objectives you will want to accomplish in your will. The following additional clauses are selected to cover some of these situations. Many form books are available to assist you if you have any other topics you wish to cover.

(1) *Devise of Family Home*

If I own a house and plot of ground at the time of my death, which is being used by me and my wife as a family home, then I give such house and plot of ground unto my wife, subject, however, to any encumbrances thereon existing at the time of my death (or free from any encumbrance thereon at the time of my death).

(2) *Bequest of Automobile*

I give unto my wife, Jane, if she shall survive me, any automobile or automobiles which I shall own at the time of my death. In the event my wife shall not survive me, then such automobile or automobiles shall be and become a part of my residuary estate.

(3) *Bequest of Household Goods*

I hereby give to my wife, Jane, all of the household goods, furnishings, and equipment located in and used by me in my home at _____ , or which at the time of my death may be located in the premises which I then occupy as my homestead.

(4) *Disinheritance of Heirs Not Name*

I have intentionally omitted all my heirs who are not specifically mentioned herein, and I hereby generally and specifically disinherit each, any, and all persons whomsoever claiming to be or who may be lawfully determined to be my heirs at law, except as otherwise mentioned in this will.

(5) *Bequest of Business*

I give and bequeath the goodwill and benefit of the business of _____ , which I am now carrying on at _____ , and also all my capital and property which shall be employed therein at my decease and also the leasehold premises situated at _____ , wherein said business is now being carried on, for all my term and interest therein, unto my son, Tim Doe, absolutely.

(6) *Division Per Stirpes*

I give and bequeath my entire estate to my children who shall survive me, their heirs, executors, administrators, and assigns, their descendants to take per stirpes and not per capita.

(7) *Division Per Capita*

Should the above named legatee predecease me, leaving children surviving me, such children shall take per capita, share and share alike, and not per stirpes.

(8) *Bequest of Unpublished Manuscripts*

I give to my son, Tim Doe all unpublished manuscripts, to be handled by him in accordance with instructions which I have given.

Execution and Witnessing of Wills

The proper signing and witnessing of your will is extremely important. Your intentions, desires and wishes are immaterial; if you do not follow the applicable statute your will may not be valid no matter what your wishes may be.

It is recommended that you make a "ceremony" out of the signing and witnessing of your will so that the witnesses will remember the occasion, that family members or persons who take under the will not act as witnesses, and that you have an extra witness if convenient.

Most statutes require at least two witnesses; some require at least three; Louisiana requires more in some circumstances. Most statutes require "competent" or "credible" witnesses; some statutes specify certain age requirements for witnesses; most do not. Some states make a devise or bequest to a witness void, with certain exceptions; some do not. A few statutes prohibit persons who have been convicted of perjury or other crimes from being competent witnesses to wills. It can be important for you to have this information available as it applies to your state.

As an extra precaution it is suggested that you follow all of the following step-by-step procedures, whether or not they are required by your state statute. These steps are included in the "ceremony" that many law offices routinely follow in the signing of wills.

Procedures for Signing and Witnessing Wills

STEP 1: Prepare the final draft of the will, preferably on a typewriter, with an original and one or more copies. Type the attestation clause in the proper place. Allow ample space for your signature and the signatures and addresses of the witnesses. Number the pages and bind them together firmly. Make certain you thoroughly understand the meaning of every part of your will.

STEP 2: Bring the witnesses together. Three witnesses will satisfy the requirements in all states except Louisiana. None of these witnesses should be related to you or your wife or husband, nor should they be anyone named in any way in your will. You and the witnesses should be in a private room with no one else in the room.

STEP 3: Inform the witnesses that the document before them is your last will. It is not necessary or even desirable that they be allowed to read it. Then you should state that you are about to sign your will and request the witnesses to witness your signature. With the witnesses watching, you should then date the will and sign your name on the line below the date.

After you have completely signed and dated the will, say to the witnesses, "This is my signature and this is my will." Then request that the witnesses sign it. You should sign only the original; the carbon copies, as a matter of good practice, remain unsigned, but conformed.

STEP 4: Have the witnesses read the attestation clause. Then have each witness sign immediately below the attestation clause and write his or her address. The witnesses should see you sign the will and you should see them sign it. Neither you nor any of the witnesses should leave the room until all have signed the document. Each signature should be observed by you and all the witnesses.

Now the document is a will. The signed original should be placed in a safe place where it is available to you and the executor. Do not place it in your safety deposit vault because a court order may be required to get it out. The unsigned copies should be placed in a different safe place for information purposes.

Holographic Wills

Some state statutes permit a person to write a valid will in his or her own handwriting with no witnesses needed; some states do not. Some of the statutes require that the will be written, dated, and signed entirely in the testator's own handwriting. Other statutes, based on the Uniform Probate Code, require only that the signature and the material provisions of the will be in the testator's handwriting. By requiring only the "material provisions" to be in the testator's handwriting, such holographic wills may be valid even though immaterial parts, such as the date or introductory wording be printed or stamped. Under these statutes a valid holographic will might even be executed on some printed will forms if the printed portion could be eliminated and the handwritten portion could evidence the testator's will. For some persons unable to obtain legal assistance, the holographic will may be adequate.

State Statutes Governing Holographic Wills

Here is a review of the state statutes governing holographic wills:

1. Holographic wills are valid where the signature and the material provisions of the will are made in the handwriting of the testator in the following states: Alaska [13.11.160], Arizona [14-2503], Colorado [15-11-503], Idaho [15-2-503], Montana [91A-2-503], Nebraska [30-2328], North Dakota [30.1-08-03], South Dakota [2-503], Tennessee [32-105], Utah [75-2-503].

2. When the entire body of the will and the signature are in the handwriting of the testator, it may be established by the evidence of at least three disinterested witnesses to the handwriting and signature of the testator, without subscribing witnesses in Arkansas [60.404].

3. A will written entirely in the testator's handwriting and signed and dated by him is valid in the following states: California [Prob. Code 53], Louisiana [C.C. 1588], Nevada [133.090], Oklahoma [84.54].

4. A holographic will is valid if it is wholly written and subscribed by the testator in the following states: Mississippi [91-5-1], Virginia [64.1-49], West Virginia [41-1-3], Wyoming [2-55].

5. A will wholly written by the testator is valid in Texas [Prob. Code 60].

A few states, notably New York, North Carolina, Rhode Island, Maryland and South Carolina, have statutes so limited in the operation of the holographic wills that they are not here reported.

For those who reside in the states listed above, the holographic will may be adequate if you execute it in accordance with your own state statutes. It is anticipated that other states will recognize the holographic will in the future.

A FREE ISSUE OF THE *CITIZEN'S LAW ADVISOR* IS WAITING FOR YOU!

Dear Friend,

Although this is the end of the book, it's just the beginning for you!

The *CITIZEN'S LAW ADVISOR* is a quarterly newspaper packed with human interest stories, advice on how readers are using the *CITIZEN'S LAW LIBRARY,* insights into tax shelters and other income sheltering and producing items, plus a complete book review and bookshelf section listing other titles in the field of layperson's law published by Prentice-Hall, Inc.

To receive your free complimentary issue of the *CITIZEN'S LAW ADVISOR* simply write your name and address on the coupon below and mail the coupon without further delay. Or call, toll-free, 1-800-228-2054 and tell the operator where you saw this announcement.

I look forward to hearing from you!

Sincerely yours,

J. Stephen Lanning

J. Stephen Lanning
Executive Vice President
Citizen's Law Library

CITIZENS LAW LIBRARY, Box 1745, 7 South Wirt Street, Leesburg, Va. 22075

Yes, please send me a free complimentary copy of the latest issue of THE CITIZENS LAW ADVISOR.

Signature _____

Name _____

Address _____

City _____ State _____ Zip _____

CGL

THE CITIZEN'S LEGAL GUIDE

The Citizen's Guide to the Law

A guide that will be useful to laymen in their everyday dealings with business, government, and the law, **The Citizen's Guide to the Law** explains • no-fault insurance • white collar crimes • the court systems • wills • partnerships • the Tax Reform Act of 1976 • estate planning • and much more. This book also talks about historical law practices such as the law of Moses, the law of ancient Greeks, and law in ancient Rome, and leads up to discussions on American, Constitutional, and Statutory Law in the 1980s.

Look for these other professional business guides from Spectrum Books!

PROBATE
NO-FAULT DIVORCE
WRITING A WILL
YOU CAN BE YOUR OWN LAWYER IN COURT
THE LANDLORD-TENANT RELATIONSHIP

John C. Howell

PRENTICE-HALL, Inc.,
Englewood Cliffs, New Jersey 07632
Cover design by Honi Werner